THE
ONE AND ONLY
LAW OF
WINNING

THE
ONE AND
ONLY
LAW OF
WINNING

BERN WHEELER

KOGAN
PAGE

First published in the United States of America in 1990 by Shapolsky Publishers Inc, 136 West 22nd Street, New York, NY 10011, USA.

This edition first published in Great Britain in 1991 by Kogan Page Ltd, 120 Pentonville Road, London N1 9JN.

British Library Cataloguing in Publication Data

A CIP record for this book is available from the British Library.

ISBN 0–7494–0453–1

Printed and bound in Great Britain by
Clays Ltd, St Ives plc

Dedication

This book is dedicated to the memory of my late father, Robert Francis Wheeler. Although he did not know the law, he pointed me towards it.

Contents

Acknowledgements   8
Introduction   9

Part 1. This is the Law   11
  1. The Law   13
  2. Why This is the Only Law   21

Part 2. Believing the Law   31
  3. Winning and Blame   33
  4. Winning and Failure   39
  5. Winning and Luck   45
  6. Winning and Confidence   51
  7. Winning and Justice   59
  8. Winning and Trust   63
  9. Winning and Risk   71

Part 3. Practising the Law   77
  10. Strength: Find it and Use it   79
  11. Attention: Pay the Full Price   91
  12. Change: Real Power is Portable   99
  13. Communication: Perceptions are Perfections . . .
     and More   105
  14. Thinking: The Wisdom of Investigation,
     Imagination and Ignorance   113
  15. Conflict: Decongest it before it Consumes You 123
  16. Authority: It Comes with the Territory   129

Part 4. Living the Law   135
  17. The Difference: Really Deciphering the Law   137
  18. A Perspective: Where You are Going   143
  19. Only You: What You Really Need   147

Further Reading from Kogan Page   150

Acknowledgements

Many contributed to this book and I am grateful to them all.

First I must acknowledge and thank the two people who challenged me to state the law and write what it means – to everyone. They are Don Davies and Greg Cochrane.

Next I thank my early readers – nine people who read an early draft of this book and gave me significant feedback. They are: Colin Acton, Ellen Gillis, Fred Harris, Peter MacKellar, David Muller, Alex Tilley, Kayleen Watson, Don Weese and Joe Wheeler.

For dedicated and detailed research I thank Jennifer Sweeney. Her efforts helped to shape the content of this book.

For preparation of this manuscript, and all that it entailed – countless revisions, long hours, constant concentration, and belief in the law – I thank my assistant, Donna Gillis.

Bern Wheeler

Introduction

You don't need most of what you've already read or heard about 'winning'. You don't need to (a) think positively, (b) act negatively, (c) unleash any secret power within you, or (d) undergo any change that wouldn't be you. You don't need to (e) imitate the latest success story from business or (f) practise any of the 'great' success theories of all time.

You don't need any of it. You need only to absorb and make use of *The One and Only Law of Winning*.

This won't necessarily be easy – even though it's waiting for you.

You are about to read a book that is different from any of the other personal and business self-help books: a book that says there is only *one* law of winning, one simple sentence that forms the fundamental truth behind *every* honest prescription for success ever spoken or written. This one law has been obscured and undermined by the armies of how-to-succeed authors who have been overzealously communicating their personal paths to success. Somehow they've missed the point that people are all different and that one person can no more follow another's exact footsteps to success any more than they can duplicate another's fingerprints.

This is the law that has been almost buried, the law that works for all people – each in his or her own way, all the time. As you will soon read, I do use my own experiences to detail and exemplify the law, but I also use those of many other people, from many walks of life, some famous, some you have never heard of. This is certainly *not* the biography of any one person. It *is* most certainly the biography of one very big, yet one very simple, idea.

How will the book help you?

This depends on what you want and what you are prepared to change within yourself in order to believe, practise, and live the One and Only Law of Winning. You will learn that this is not only a law in the commercial sense – a law that heralds a Donald Trump and ignores a Mother Teresa. Although the law has and will continue to be used to earn a great deal of money, it is also a law of life. This being so, you will be able to live *The One and Only Law of Winning* for your own winning results now and, as you wish, for the rest of your life.

Bern Wheeler
Toronto, Canada
1990

Part 1

This is the Law

Everyone who wins does so with his or her own techniques, personality, talent, character and ambition – yet using the same law.

There are many ways of winning, but there is only one law. You are about to learn it, as simply as I believe it can be expressed.

CHAPTER 1

The Law

After you have read this book your world may be very different. It is my sincere hope that some time in the future you will face an opportunity, challenge (or problem) and, in at least a partial reflection of what you read here, you will say calmly to someone or even to yourself, 'It's all right; I know exactly what I have to do.'

Of course I don't know when or if that will happen, but I believe it is very possible, even if you've opened this book with a healthy degree of scepticism. You see, the law is only eight words long (we're coming to them), and by weighing those eight words and what they mean to you against whatever circumstances you face – you will actually be practising the law.

I realise I will be taking a risk in stating the law in eight simple words. Others might have explained it as a complicated and twisting theory full of sophisticated language, revelling in its slow recitation, one sentence at a time over several chapters. Not me. The words and concepts are easy.

The challenge comes in both absorbing and practising the law, since it seems to be just a simple sentence. My risk in simplifying this theory into eight words is that I will lose *your* interest and *my* credibility. At first these eight words may elicit your scorn, a smirk, a shrug, or at best a questioning scratch of the head. I strongly doubt that any revelation will unfold. You may not even understand them. Not even at the end of this chapter, or the next, when I explain why this is the only law, do I expect you to comprehend them fully. At best, I'll have your curiosity hooked; it's the rest of the book that will either convince you or not.

By now you may well be thinking, 'All right, all right. What are these eight words that I won't understand right away but are so important? Tell me and I'll decide how important they are.'

Let me try your patience for just one more thought.

Why is this One and Only Law of Winning a law? Why isn't it a principle? A method? Or just a rule? Why a law? The answer is in the effect that the law is already having on your life whether you believe it or practise it or not. It is demanding of your belief, is ruthless if disregarded and relentless in its results – yet, so profitable when obeyed. That's why it is a law and, in reality, the only law of winning.

Are you ready now?

The One and Only Law of Winning is:

ONLY CONSTANT SELF-CONFRONTATION OF RESPONSIBILITY REAPS RESULTS.

So what's the big deal? you ask. Wouldn't the Boy Scouts' motto be just as profound? Wouldn't any one of a hundred clichés about success be just as true? No, they wouldn't.

Only constant self-confrontation of responsibility reaps results. In those eight words you'll find the foundation of all human success. In those eight words you'll find the true motivation of all time. In those eight words you'll find – if you look long enough, and hard enough – the truth about what you can become, the goals you can accomplish, how you will be rewarded. It's all there, and each of the eight words contributes to the complete law.

What follows is a quick dissection of the law and the importance of its component parts. Read first Lee Iacocca's comments on his reaction to the sorry state of Chrysler when he arrived to take over as president: 'When times get tough, there's no choice except to take a deep breath, carry on, and do the best you can.'[1]

Ho-hum, you say. What's so special about that? Just shoulder-to-the-wheel, let's-get-the-job-done talk, isn't it? Yes, it is, but only on the surface. In its depth is the beginning of a definition of the word 'responsibility'. By the time you finish this book you will discover that your definition of that word will also define, more than anything else, how much you will accomplish in life.

Let's move from motor city to the film mecca: Hollywood, California. Elizabeth Taylor said of her decision to enter the Betty

Ford clinic for alcohol and drug dependence: 'It's a question of self-worth, of self-esteem. I had the desire finally to clean up my act. It all just clicked in my head.'[2]

What was responsibility worth to Ms Taylor until she made the important self-confrontation, the 'click' in her own head about her own worth and esteem? By the time you finish this book, you may find that something clicks in *your* head that will give a new meaning to the words 'self-confrontation'.

On to Paterson, New Jersey, where school headteacher Joe Clark made educational history by constantly confronting the crime-ridden and graffiti-infested inner city school of 3200 students when he arrived there in 1982. His tough and determined measures included banning pupils from loitering, setting up a dress code and punishing lateness and class cutting with graffiti-cleaning duty. He was very successful in bringing education back to his school. Clark said, 'Discipline is the ultimate tenet of education. Discipline establishes the format, the environment for academic achievement to occur.'[3]

What is discipline, I ask you, but a constant condition? You don't need a dictionary for your own definition, but by the time you finish reading this book you may react to the word 'constant' in a different way.

Remember: *only constant self-confrontation of responsibility reaps results*.

We move thousands of miles away, to a Soviet concentration camp in Siberia. It was there that Natan Sharansky – mathematician, computer scientist, and dissident – was sentenced to a prison camp under false charges in 1979. Through degradation and torture at the hands of his captors, Sharansky never broke. After his release in 1986, he wrote that in prison he formulated this principle to live by:

Nothing they do can humiliate me. I alone can humiliate myself.[4]

Have you read something similar, so far in this book? Sharansky goes on:

Once I had absorbed that idea, nothing – not searches, not

punishment, not even several attempts to force-feed me through the rectum during an extended hunger strike – could deprive me of my self-respect.

You are not a prisoner in a Soviet prison camp. You are not a headteacher of an inner city school. You are not a film star. Nor are you the chairman of a major corporation. It doesn't matter. What matters is that there is an idea presented to you in this chapter and, like Mr Sharansky's idea, it too has to be *absorbed* to be effective in your life. And it can be.

What do you want?

- Do you want to grow a new business?

- Do you want to earn more money?

- Do you want to communicate better with someone you love?

- Do you want to lose weight? To gain weight?

- Improve your body?

- Become successful?

You don't have to have a high-powered job or super status to live the law. You only have to believe it and, like Natan Sharansky, to absorb the law and practise it.

Earla Vaters, the *Toronto Globe and Mail* reported, is a woman who, one year before June 1988, was (a) grossly overweight, (b) living on social security, (c) verbally abusing her children, and (d) suffering from agoraphobia, one of the most disabling phobias, one that instils panic attacks so severe that Mrs Vaters said, 'I couldn't get on a bus, I couldn't go into a store.'[5]

Doctors confirmed the severity of this phobia, but Mrs Vaters' own words serve perfectly. 'Your heart pounds and you can hardly breathe. Something the size of a golfball seems stuck in your throat. You are sure that in the next minute you will go insane. Or die.'

Globe and Mail columnist June Callwood told the story of how with patient effort, through the help of a psychologist who taught her how to relax and from a group called Friends and Advocates who compassionately worked with her for more than a year, Mrs Vaters overcame the obstacle of her phobia, actually went to work for Friends and Advocates, came off social security, lost weight, and made her family proud of her.

She did not overcome it all. She still has panic attacks but has learned how to work through them. And she has become a winner.

Callwood, unlike most writers of such a story, started her column without mentioning Mrs Vaters or her problem. She began with an insightful and powerful paragraph stating:

Adults have to grow by themselves; there's no other way. However helpful the therapists, or medication, or encouragement from the near and dear, emotional maturity is homemade. People arrive at homeostasis by a process that often begins with desperation, and is assisted by a scrap of spunkiness that fortuitously floats by in a drowning sea. People can decide they will be happy, and then become it.

To some, the One and Only Law of Winning will be the catalyst to an almost dormant 'scrap of spunkiness' and the process of absorbing this book will be likened to a boat that 'fortuitously floats by in a drowning sea'. For others it will be different and the law will be accepted as a rational idea they will add to – no, they will absorb into – an already-winning life and use to their further advantage.

Yet others will absorb nothing because they are looking for some sort of magical improvement in their lives, not a law to be practised. They are already so stuck on seeking easy solutions to life's problems through instant remedies that anything as simple as the law will float right by them.

I would now like to tell you how I evolved those eight rational words of winning, and what they have meant to me.

As I write this book, I am a 45-year-old businessman, owner of a special-project advertising agency. But as much as anything, I am a student of motivation and communication. *How* and *why* people succeed and fail in life has always fascinated me and I have read all the relevant books, or at least as many as I could get my hands on. Most of the ideas on the subject were different: there are more angles on winning than there are on a compass.

Even allowing for a high percentage of hocum, there were many well-thought-out and documented theories on winning. Could they all be right? Or wrong? I wasn't sure.

About eight or nine years ago, I saw a successful businessman interviewed on television. His was in many ways a typical rags-to-riches story: an immigrant who arrived from Hitler's concentration camps with nothing and built a thriving business empire. I saw the interview by chance and did not think I would remember it – probably because he appeared to be, in his presentation, the antithesis of what I believed winning was all about. I recall that more than anything, he appeared boorish. An East European accent made him difficult to understand and he had an aggravating guttural laugh that ridiculed the questions he was asked. His manner on television was, to me, downright annoying.

When asked about competition, after his guttural laugh, he answered, 'Competition? Where I come from the competition wanted to put me in an oven. Over here they just don't want me to make the sale. Competition here is easy.'

I had no desire to remember that interview, but I did – specifically the surprising comment on competition; a haunting reminder of his image.

A few years later, I was deeply moved by something on a totally unrelated subject. It was the perception of pain felt by people who had identical injuries caused by car accidents. The statistics were related to the cause of the accident: when another driver was at fault, the pain suffered was 40 per cent greater than when there was no one else to blame for the accident.

I would like to report that I received a great catharsis of understanding from this realisation, that a light went on in my head, and that the law was suddenly revealed. Unfortunately this was not the case. But those two observations, the successful immigrant's story and the statistics on pain perception, locked in my mind over time. They both had a common denominator, an essential truth of life; of that I became convinced.

It was months later that I felt compelled to think about and confront both experiences, together with everything I had read and believed about winning:

Everyone was a little bit right in their ideas about winning, but everyone was also a little bit wrong. There is only one essential component to winning, one focus. Once you define yourself by your responsibility, and once everything you believe you do relates to that, nothing else matters. The person who feels less pain after the car accident does so because he or she has accepted responsibility for recovery. The immigrant businessman at one time had the responsibility of avoiding death on a daily basis. Once your competition wants literally to kill you, other competitors who just don't want you to sell are really easy – but only if you accept beating your competition as your responsibility!

Was that really all there was to it? Were attitude (thinking positively) and organisation (planning your work and working your plan, or any of the other formulas for success) all unnecessary for success? Yes, I answered, they are only unnecessary if you really don't need them, if you don't accept them as your responsibility. There is just one thing, among all the other popular ideas on winning, that counts.

I started to apply the One and Only Law of Winning to my life and business. I had never considered income the priority of my business. The idea of being a small, special-project agency where I was personally involved in all projects was more important to me than creating a larger, possibly more profitable company. Yet I found that my business did become more profitable in every way. Priorities became simple, problems were solved sooner, and my personal income catapulted.

All because of the law?

Yes. But not just by saying it, or believing it. By practising it and by living it. The rest of this book is a report on how not just I, but every winner, does just that.

In the next chapter I challenge all the theories and stories of success ever devised or communicated. You'll read why I believe that all the ideas that work boil down to the same thing: the basic law that cannot be boiled down or reduced in any way – *The One and Only Law of Winning.*

Notes

1. Lee Iacocca with William Novak (1986) *Iacocca: An Autobiography*, Bantam.
2. *Ladies' Home Journal*, November 1987.
3. *Time*, 7 February 1988.
4. Natan Sharansky (1988) *Fear No Evil*, Random House.
5. *Toronto Globe and Mail*, 15 June 1988.

CHAPTER 2

Why This is the Only Law

A part of me wanted to dedicate this book to the many thousands of acres of trees that have been sacrificed to make the many books that have told us how to be winners and successful – so many times over. And, I shouldn't forget the millions of feet of audiotape, and videotape, now being spun to serve the same purpose.

Winning is a booming and prosperous industry.

But can all the books and tapes be right? Why do the people of the world still have so many problems when there are all those 'formulas for success' out there? Would the trees that made those books have perhaps served us better if they'd been left to blow in the wind? But I digress.

I have a very simple mission in this chapter: I must show you how all the theories of winning that work for anyone, even those that are seemingly contradictory, share a common premise: the One and Only Law of Winning.

My mission requires another question, though. If the eight words that define the One and Only Law of Winning are so simple, why has no one put them on paper before? I believe the answer is that the law is too simple and devoid of mystique, unlike the 'systems' for success that authors have been churning out for decades. A part of all of us likes things simple, but if someone juices up simplicity with personal packaging, gives it a complete, detailed formula with more steps to follow and fewer thoughts to think about, isn't that a more appealing package?

The last thing I want to turn this book into is a boring lesson on the history of how-to-win publications. And I won't. But I do have to stake out very clearly my own justification for why this is the *only* law of winning, and to do this I have to give you a quick overview of the types of books that have come before.

I group all how-to-win books into four categories: the inspirational, the hostile, the irrational, and the biographical.

Inspirational

These are the grandparents of how-to-win books, exemplified by Norman Vincent Peale in his series of 'positive thinking' books. Each is rooted in the nineteenth-century positivist philosophy of French psychotherapist Emile Coué. These types of book share two unshakeable fundamentals for success: faith and persistence. Sometimes the faith is spiritual in nature, sometimes it's not. Each is loaded with testimonial after testimonial of those who believed in a specific positive-thinking system and overcame great obstacles in order to become winners.

Hostile

These are get-the-other-person-before-he-or-she-gets-you books, and they have great appeal to those who believe that they have at some time been beaten by the system or any segment of society. They each propose a tough and individualistic formula of non-trust and looking out for yourself in order to get ahead and win.

Irrational

In books of this type there is a secret power to be unleashed from within the readers, if they can only tap their full potential. (There is usually some reference to people like Shakespeare or Einstein, tapping only 10 per cent of their true potential.) To find this power, the readers are usually provided with a special formula to tap their subconscious mind – which is lurking just below everyday conscious awareness, with all the knowledge and wisdom needed to attain success.

Biographical

These are really how-to-win books by association rather than by direct intent. Successful lives are profiled, as either biographies or autobiographies, and readers are invited to capture insight and wisdom from someone who has already made it to the top rung of the ladder of success.

In reverse order I will now examine where each of the four types of winning book goes wrong in its assumptions and prescriptions of success for the masses.

Biographical types are exempted from 'going wrong' because they don't normally try to win converts. They are written from the top of the hill, after the winning has been done, and each book has a winner's ego-driven slant on reality, on his or her own proven way of winning. We don't read these books to find any system to win with; rather, we read these books for either good gossip to enjoy or quick wisdom to extract and tack on to our own lives. Or both.

And what do we find? Buried among the variables of every individual's experiences we find intelligence, ideas, opportunities, crises, persistence, and both bad and good luck. When we read these books thoroughly and analytically there emerges a clear sense of personal responsibility for a challenge or vision and a constant self-confrontation of the problems that cause us to avoid or only partially accept that responsibility. In the end, the confronter always overcomes the problems, reaps results, and wins. Does that sentence sound familiar?

Except, of course, that we're not expecting to find the One and Only Law there. We read these books easily and comfortably and soon get caught up in the saga of the author's experience: the personalities, the conflicts and the times. Yet the common thread in them all is the One and Only Law of Winning. You'll find it in various parts of the Lee Iacocca book mentioned in Chapter 1, and you'll also find it in most of the other biographical works. From sports heroes to scientists, from rock stars to astronauts, the law I have identified comprises an idea expressed in its eight words that transcends them all.

The irrational type of winning book can be considered a branch of the inspirational type of how-to-win book – but with a distinct difference. Yes, there is faith and positive thinking involved. However, in calling on a power to be unleashed or unshackled from the subconscious, the authors of these works are actually creating a metaphor and a source for self-confidence and, in reality, responsibility that (they assume) the reader cannot find in his or her conscious self. I believe this type of book appeals to those most in need of confidence as a springboard for action to get things done.

To the extent that the reader buys into the idea, and learns to know and confront responsibility constantly, this type of book can be beneficial. Some books do this very well, but they are at the same time flawed, for three reasons. First, most of us cannot accept a hocus-pocus appeal to a mystical power within – it's just not real. Second, on an operational level I do not see how such a 'power' can help but become a source for irresponsibility when things go wrong. Can we perhaps say, 'My subconscious made me do it' – or, 'not do it'? Can irresponsibility really be seconded to something that is not conscious and still be called responsibility?

Lastly, these types of book are not only simplistic in their systems for winning, but they are also usually shallow in their very definitions. They seem to see winning only as something to be achieved rather than a process to be lived.

The hostile type of winning book is flawed in a different but similar way. I liken this type of success approach to a three-stage rocket that is loaded with extra-high-octane fuel – but only in the first stage. The other two stages are empty. Yet it's very easy to see the appeal of this type of emotional work. The image of the outsider, one person standing alone in the face of adversity, is epitomised here. And it can certainly work in seeming to harness one's constant self-confrontation of responsibility.

With a sense of mission, the zealot in this type of book can create tremendous energy and produce exceptional work because, with the whole world dead set against him, he feels so responsible for his own success. So he soars! But there is also a very basic flaw here. The responsibility this type of book preaches is really a form of personal righteousness much like that of a crusader. He or she lives with the belief that the people that must be dealt with are the enemy. And an enemy is certainly someone to heap a lot of blame on.

But how do you really heap blame and constantly confront your own responsibility? How long before winning becomes whining and your enemies become the reason for losing?

Only a very few can ride solo to the top without the consideration or assistance of others. For most people, being seen as a major contributor to solving a problem or taking advantage of an opportunity is very often the heart of both leading and winning. For winning, winning long term – whether you're in business, a profession, or a trade, whether you're trying to sell someone something or trying to prove your own worth as a human being – you will eventually need others' support. It is a hard landing for anyone when the fuel runs out and the sky is only full of enemies.

This brings me to the inspirational type of winning book, and there is no doubt about the impact of this type of how-to-win philosophy. I believe more people have been helped by believing in it, and more people have failed because of their belief in it, than all the other categories of how-to-win books put together. Packed with clichés, this is 'every day in every way I'm growing better and better.' This is 'persistence overcoming resistance.' This is 'faith moving mountains' and the home of every dark cloud sheltering a silver lining. This is eternal hope for the hopeless and new faith for those who have lost whatever faith they previously had.

And it works. For some people it really works. But not for everyone. For others, it's a disaster. There are two reasons why this type of winning can be encouraged for some and cautioned for others.

1. Personalities cannot be adapted to zeal

A few years ago, I had an idea for a book I never pursued writing. The title was *New Hope for Positive, Cheerful People!* The subtitle was 'Now You Can Be Liked for Yourself Even Though You're Always Happy and Sickeningly Sweet'. All right, the book was going to be a good-natured put-on and a put-down. But there was, in the idea for that book, the basis for the point I'm making here: Some people have a natural disposition towards thinking and feeling positive about other people and events. These are, in my experience, the same people who like to rise early, eat hearty breakfasts, and find most babies and furry animals excessively cute. They can rise to any challenge and adapt quickly to confronting their responsibility on a daily basis.

There is a second group who benefit from a prescription of positivism. These are people who are confused but latently positive, and who discover that such belief medicine organises their behaviour to push themselves further and, more than anything, confront their responsibilities and opportunities. These are fruit ripe for the picking by the right positive system.

Then there are the rest of us. We know we would be better off if we could think and feel that way. We know we would be more productive, better liked, contribute more to relationships, and in some small way make the world a better place if we could only think and feel like that. But we would be living a lie. It's not that we're really negative; on certain occasions, and for certain interests, we can be as positive as the next person. But as a way of life, as a personal perspective on reality, it just isn't us. It's not that we lack imagination or enthusiasm. It's simply that we place a higher priority on being ourselves, on living our own personalities, on seeing the world with an honest perception of what reality is.

People who buy into any of the inspirational systems for success – without the innate or latent personality of a natural believer – wear a mask that doesn't fit. This is often found in salespeople, and the most frequent comment you hear after such a person leaves the room is: 'Is he serious?' Better to be a natural realist or even a pessimist than a fake and shallow optimist.

You must be *yourself*. That is the bottom line for all of us. That doesn't mean we cannot and should not change and improve our lives. But the change has to come from within, as a natural growth and education of who we are. Attitude and our individual view of the world cannot be implanted into us with any hope of lasting success.

2. The natural contradiction between believing and confronting

This reason is just as important as the first for being wary of inspirational success. The heart of all systems of this type, after all (to one degree or another), is faith, faith, faith. Believe, believe, believe. While faith is necessary to achieve every goal, so is evaluation (analysis of new circumstances) and the ability to change (adapt to new circumstances). This means constant self-confrontation and this is where the inspirational-type dogma falls apart for many people. It is difficult, if not impossible, for some believers to acknowledge that they can be making mistakes – even major blunders – in their lives. Life is just too positive and if they follow the prescribed programme they simply must succeed.

Consider, for instance, the salesperson who faces five, six, maybe seven rejections in a row. If the forces of positivism convince that man or woman to believe that the eighth prospect will probably be a sale and it isn't, but then the ninth probably will, where do things stop before self-confrontation takes place about how he or she should be working better (or smarter) and not harder?

In reality, experience and results, those unforgetting teachers, have to live alongside positivism, the constantly forgiving and rationalising dogma. If, after a period of following the promised programme, your results are negative, your experiences with the system will eventually demonstrate the contradiction between what you both learn and feel and the dogma you keep feeding yourself.

Which is the lie? Which is the truth?

One of the most successful salespeople I've ever known is hardly a positive-type personality. He is sincere but quiet and you would probably think him to be an accountant if you had to guess his occupation. I asked him if he had any great hurdle to overcome in his career. His answer surprised me: 'I had a hard time handling rejection,' he said.

'It really got to me. I knew the numbers said I could be quite successful if six out of seven people I talked to slammed the door in my face. But getting that door slammed in my face was slamming me, personally. So I invented a dual personality to protect myself.

Every morning I looked in the mirror, I learned to see myself as two people. I saw the surface me – the person people who don't know me think I am – and I also saw the real me. I had to see both people every morning and then to understand that though no one would reject the real me, some people will reject the person they think I am. Once I realised that people weren't rejecting the real me, I never had a problem handling rejection.'

Now, that wasn't very positive. But it was very self-confrontational.

In the big picture there is a constant confusion that haunts many positive thinkers in their daily work and personal lives. Because they are so positive, so sincere, they fail to understand the veneer that masks so many relationships. They really believe that someone important 'will get back to them soon', that people usually say what they mean. Casual comments are interpreted as actual commitments. Positive believers do not often accept the fact that nice people would rather casually lie or at least avoid saying 'no' than confront a negative decision. They programme themselves to believe otherwise; to see the next big sale in every new interaction.

Years ago, I was driving with my boss, the successful owner of the company I worked for. The subject of a potential problem in our business, one that was at that time still over the horizon and might not even touch us, came up. He was quite worried about it, he told me, and he rambled on about why. I couldn't get very excited because it was too far away and might never come close to us. 'Can't you be an optimist about it?' I asked him. I'll never forget his answer. 'Bern,' he said, 'optimists drive Mercedes; pessimists drive Datsuns'. He was driving me home at the time, in his car, a Datsun.

Was he right? Is being negative a more powerful tool for self-confrontation? Not necessarily. I've seen optimists who drive Datsuns and plenty of pessimists who drive Mercedes. But

I've never seen a winner who didn't drive himself or herself to understand and confront his or her responsibilities.

Attitude, by itself, certainly cannot make you a winner. Even the genius of your ambitious ideas and the reach of your unique talents can't make you a winner. Not by themselves.

And don't look to organised systems for an answer. I've known winners who are meticulously organised and winners who couldn't see their desk because of the confusion of paperwork on it. I've known winners who are fat and skinny, young and old, male and female, black, white, and yellow, silver-tongued and stammer-prone, religious and non-religious, moral and immoral. I've known winners who dress like a millionaire and others who dress as if they haven't got a penny.

What does it all prove? Simply that there is no system for winning that has universal application, because people are just too different. Each of the systems of winning can be effective, at least in the short term, if the system matches the belief system and attitude of the believer. But at their hearts all the best winning systems say that you must take responsibility for your life and make it happen. That is all. *That is everything!*

The only thing all winners have in common is the law: only constant self-confrontation of responsibility reaps results. Yet most winners, even those who don't read how-to books, don't know that they're practising the One and Only Law. They think that they are successful because of their own unique, individual approach to life. This common denominator that unites them is always ignored. It shouldn't be; it should be shared.

I hope I have been successful in my mission for this chapter: getting you to agree that the heart of every winning system is the same, regardless of packaging. My next challenge, in the balance of this book, is much greater. It is to reveal the depth of the law and show you that it is also a law of life, that the One and Only Law of Winning is working for or against everyone, including you, right now.

Part 2

Believing the Law

Winners have common beliefs about seven key concepts of living and working. These concepts have a very direct relationship to the One and Only Law of Winning.

In the following chapters I not only explore these concepts but challenge you to confront your own beliefs about each of them.

This is important.

CHAPTER 3

Winning and Blame

My friend leaned over the table at the bar we were in and reflected a profound, if exaggerated, thought. Just hours before, he had been involved in an ugly and painful divorce and custody incident in his family. It was weighing heavily on his mind.

'You know,' he said, 'if people could ever take the energy they use in hating and blaming each other for screwing up each other's lives, and devote that energy somehow to cancer research, the disease could probably be cured in six weeks.'

He was wrong. It would take a little longer, but he was right in the direction his thought was taking him. This is the essence of the One and Only Law of Winning.

We are all affected by the level of energy we apply to anything we do in order to achieve what we want. I don't want to get into a dispute with scientists about the source and expenditure of energy, but I can certainly safely make this observation about human energy: it swells from desire, is limited to various degrees in all people, and how it is used determines what is accomplished in life.

Those who use their energy blaming others, regardless of fault, limit the potential of their lives more than they ever know. Winners, I have observed, have a perception and belief about the word 'blame' that is different from other people's. They live, without really understanding it themselves, what I call a 'no-fault life'.

What is a no-fault life? Is it a life where no blame is assessed? Where justice is not sought? Where wrong is not righted?

No, it isn't. Winners, just like everyone else, do assess blame, seek justice, and right wrongs. But what is truly different about winners is that the subject of personal justice (the unfairness of life) never consumes them. They somehow know that if it did, they would be detached from whatever goal that is propelling them ahead. They believe, innately or from life's experiences, that they must take responsibility for the circumstances they face and demote blame (anyone or anything who caused their problems) to a lower plateau. Usually they forget about or ignore blame altogether.

This is an easier concept to write about than to practise, I know, especially in today's world, where the tendency is to do just the opposite.

Blame has been escalated throughout the judicial systems in the West, none more so than in the US where many doctors will not stop in the street to treat an accident victim because of fear of dangerous lawsuits for negligence. Here in the UK the courts are full with all manner of lawsuits and the media regularly report libel, industrial negligence and an increasing number of medical malpractice cases.

Is it better for a company or local council to settle lawsuits for massive amounts of money (which it will have to pass along through price or tax increases), even when it believes it is not at fault – because if it loses in court, it might not be able to get future insurance? Is it right that doctors should face the growing moral dilemma in medicine?

Not long ago, society's matters of right and wrong were determined by a simple moral code. There was only one and it was simple. It was generally grounded on that ever-important word 'responsibility'. Not any more. It is now decided by the various courts and by fear. The influx of information available to us on who did what, how, when, where and why has never been greater. When we've been wronged, we seek this information and use it in the pursuit of justice. We have now created a massive, legal network of bureaucracy for blame and value appropriation. And everyone sucked into the network is encouraged to seek justice predominantly in one way: in the judgement of currency, hard cash.

The situation is not easy for anyone, least of all the courts. What is an arm worth? A career? A life? How much should a family be awarded that has lost a breadwinner, when the future holds uncertain the rate of inflation? If the breadwinner and the sued were equally at fault, should the sued party (eg, an insurance company) pay more because it has the resources to pay whereas the family may be penniless? When does justice become wealth redistribution because it seems right, rather than weighed dispassionately on the scales of responsibility?

I do not want you to think, through this mini-tirade, that I am blaming the lawyers, courts or justice seekers. Nor am I condoning faulty products that cause injury or irresponsible behaviour that results in tragedy. I am not saying you should not use the courts to seek justice.

I am merely commenting on the temper of the times. If the courts have become a massive, legal network of blame and value appropriation, what have day-to-day relationships become for so many people? How many people blame the circumstances of their lives on their job, boss, husband, wife, children, father, mother, town or city, client, customers, partner, associate, even the weather? And maybe, even worse, how many blame themselves and let guilt or bitterness – whichever emotion arises in the heart first – dominate their lives?

The answer, of course, to these last two questions is: too many.

But not winners. The actress who has been libelled by the downmarket tabloid is incensed, sues the publication, but doesn't let the litigation interfere with the pursuit of her career. The athlete or coach who loses in the big race or game because of his or her own or someone else's fault is temporarily crushed with disappointment. However, before despair takes a permanent hold, he or she would be wise to formulate a comeback plan. Blame has to take a backseat, or it would drive winners into a future they rightfully refuse to get bogged down with.

This may be the most difficult confrontation to make, for it requires you to accept that, yes, justice should prevail, everyone should be held responsible for his or her actions – but that a focus on blame should not be a motivator in your life. The cause of your life should be taking responsibility for what's in front of you now, no matter who or what caused your present life circumstances.

Only by doing so will you live a no-fault life.

The challenge for me is to make you want to make that essential confrontation with what you believe about blame. A series of examples about other people's experiences and beliefs might not hit home. You see, it's easy for any 'how-to' writer to fall into the habit of reciting story after story, example after example, of his or her truth. To the writer, every story is more ammunition better to hit the target, dead-weight proof to convince the reader. However, if the subject is discomforting, I don't believe the reader interprets the same way as the writer writes. The reader, if he enjoys the book, digests stories the same way he digests Chinese food. He gobbles them all up and isn't sure an hour later what he actually consumed. He just knows he enjoyed it. As far as real confrontation is concerned, readers usually react by feeling, 'Yes, they were great stories, but they're not me.'

I'm not going to try to find you – because I can't. You have to find yourself. Only you are responsible for that self-confrontation about your life and only you can choose to live a no-fault life.

> *Only constant self-confrontation of*
> *responsibility reaps results*

Blame and You:

Essential Self-Confrontations

- Winners lead a no-fault life. They self-confront their own responsibilities for their life circumstances. Do you?

- To lead a no-fault life, winners ignore or even banish blame. Do you?

- Winners define their own responsibilities as a priority of life. In doing so they form the beginning of a plan of action. Do you?

CHAPTER 4

Winning and Failure

Until recently, failure was a word most people would rather choke on than apply to themselves. Failures were previously called 'setbacks', 'reverses', and 'negative experiences'. The word failure itself was too difficult to handle, for it had a terminal ring to it.

Not any more. Failure has become a very accepted and 'in' word these days. From pschoanalysts' couches to business books, all the way to corporate boardrooms, people are encouraged to calculate, enunciate, and sometimes even celebrate their failures as though they were inverted successes.

Are they? How do winners perceive failure, handle failure, and also, dispose of failure? What should you believe about failure in order to practise the One and Only Law of Winning?

If, picking up from the last chapter, you take responsibility squarely on your shoulders and lead a no-fault life, you may believe I'm going to advise you to deal with failure in the same way. I'm not. In an important way, failure is something you should actually analyse thoroughly – but not for a long period, and seldom in any public way.

Blame is perception of responsibility, but failure is 'judgement of an event'. This definition of failure comes from *When Smart People Fail* by Carole Hyatt and Linda Gottlieb, a remarkable book on the subject of failure.[1] The authors interviewed 200 people from different walks of life about analysing failure and how to turn it around. If you find yourself in any way stuck on this subject, or are just interested in it, by all means buy this book. The title is misleading; *When Smart People Fail* is as much about winning as it is about failing.

Failures are not inverted successes but are stepping stones to success, and winners do handle and dispose of failure faster than other people simply because it is such an intense part of our lives. According to one businessman, failure is 'what we all do best'.

The gurus, however, seem to have missed a critical aspect of confronting and learning from failure. And that is to start small. Start with the irritating, pesky failures that crowd our every day: the traffic light we thought we would get through before it turned red; the project we were sure we would finish before we went home; the sale we were sure we would make before the month ended. This list of little failures could be endless, but let me stop here. If we didn't have ambition, and expectations, we wouldn't have failures. Therefore, the greater our ambitions and expectations are in life, the more we will certainly fail.

The problem with many people is the way minor failures are rationalised away. 'If that driver in front of me hadn't turned, I'd have made that light.' 'If the phone had stopped ringing, I'd have finished that project.' 'If the new buyer hadn't replaced the usual buyer, I'd have made that sale.' There is a reason for everything, grounded in blame (rather than in self-confrontation of responsibility that can turn failure from bitter rationalisation into personal learning).

Yes, failure – to winners – is not losing. It's learning. Consider the same minor failing scenarios handled with just a touch of rationalisation but with much self-confrontational reality: 'I didn't make the damn light! I'd better learn to leave earlier if traffic is going to be this bad.' 'These calls are driving me up the wall! Either I take no more calls till this project is done, work late, or finish it later in the week. Something has to change.' 'What a waste of time presenting to that new buyer. I'd probably better realise I can't always sell our line of products to that account. I'll have to concentrate more on my other accounts if I am to maintain my present level of commission.'

For three very good reasons, it is critically important to confront small failures:

1. Resolving to change

You move into an action mode that creates change or a resolution to change and away from a stale mode of complaining. Talk is still the cheapest currency in the land: if you don't leave earlier, stop taking calls, concentrate on selling to your other accounts . . . . If you don't take some action beyond complaining, you'll feel worse for knowing what has to be done and not doing it.

2. Small failures can mushroom quickly

If not confronted very directly, these failures may have a way of growing beyond the object of blame – the car in front of you, the ringing telephone, the new buyer. They become very big and get lumped together with other failures to form a vivid image of defeat. Direct confrontation cuts feelings of defeat short and allows you to move on to the next challenge.

3. There are only two types of failure

There are minor failures and there are major failures, but there are no medium-sized failures. Two sizes, and just two sizes fit all people. And major failure is almost impossible to escape. You could lose a job, a business, or see a long-term relationship self-destruct before your eyes. But winners who enforce the One and Only Law are very different in how they deal with major failure simply because of the conditioning that self-confrontation of minor failure brings. Winners take action rapidly when they fail. It becomes a habit they do not forget.

In *When Smart People Fail*, authors Hyatt and Gottlieb analyse the anatomy of major career failures – loss of job, failure of business, and so on – in terms of the stages we go through to realise we can start again. Hyatt and Gottlieb say these are: (a) shock, (b) fear, (c) anger and blame, (d) shame, and (e) despair. They believe that people go through these stages at various speeds, some very quickly. They succinctly add that 'others seem never to complete the cycle, remaining stuck in their own failures, victims of disordered mourning, vainly feeling what is forever gone'.

41

If you accept constant self-confrontation of responsibility as a way of life, the speed at which you find yourself passing through these stages, and perhaps avoiding or at least merging some, will amaze even you.

Joe Sugarman, mail-order entrepreneur, earned millions when he sold electronic calculators and other electronic gadgetry in the 1970s and early 1980s. Anyone who asked Joe the secret of his success got the same answer. 'I failed my way to success,' he said. When I spoke to him, I found that this was not a quick cliché answer but a fact based on a very tough, dispassionate analysis of every venture he developed, every mail-order ad he wrote. No fire officer ever went through the ashes of a burned-down building with more scrutiny than Sugarman went through the ashes of his failures, looking for clues about what did go right besides what went wrong and why.

Confronting major failures is harder than the minor ones because we realise that everyone is well aware of our big failures. But there is no way out of this.

Listen to what Pat Riley, coach of basketball team the Los Angeles Lakers, has to say on this subject:

'If you go about living your life as you choose, and you're happy with it, and you're on a mission, then the opinion-makers will never really affect you. I think it comes down to defining the discipline in your life, the character in your life, the quality of your life.'[2]

He goes on, commenting on his own recuperation from the Lakers' big loss in 1984:

'I went through torment that summer, being publicly mocked and humiliated by the media. But I realized that it didn't make any difference, what had happened. What matters is how you deal with it. It's how you take it. It's how you come back from it.'

'Coming back from it' is the secret of so many successes. Henry Ford started two motor-car companies that were both failures before he created the Ford Motor Company which exists today.

How many hundred filaments did Thomas Edison fail with until he finally invented the electric light? The history of every success is laden with many failures, and no one starts at the top and instantly learns from one major failure. You have to learn how to start with your minor failures.

Accepting the minor failure is what we all do best. I add that failure is also what we experience more frequently. There are more red lights than green lights, more minor disappointments than great exultations in life. We savour the wins and obliterate the failures. But when we fail, we must be prepared to learn and, wherever possible, take corrective action for the future quickly and decisively.

That is what the One and Only Law of Winning demands, and there is no doubt whatsoever that such action will prepare you for the really big failures – and yes, for an even greater education as you both enforce and practise the law.

Notes

1. Carole Hyatt and Linda Gottlieb (1987) *When Smart People Fail*, Simon and Schuster.
2. *Esquire*, June 1988.

> *Only constant self-confrontation of*
> *responsibility reaps results*

Failure and You:

Essential Self-Confrontations

- Winners acknowledge that they will experience more failures in life, large and small, than successes. Do you?

- Winners believe that failure isn't losing. It's learning. Do you?

- Winners learn best from failures by starting small, by taking action to relieve the annoying, small failures we all encounter. This prepares winners to deal better with life's larger failures. Do you do this?

CHAPTER 5

Winning and Luck

In this chapter I have good news, bad news, and real news.

First, the good news: You are one lucky person.

Next, the bad news: Your luck is both good and bad.

And now, the real news: if you are more than six years old, 85 per cent of your luck, both good or bad, has already come your way. And guess what: it wasn't fair!

Yes, dear reader, a great percentage of your make-up – intelligence, looks, disposition, talent, and even life expectancy – was decided without any consideration of your worth as a person. It was decided by your genes. And a great deal of your very identity – your confidence, ambition, and attitude – was heavily influenced by the environment in which you were raised, especially the first few years. The Jesuits have a saying: 'Give us a child until he is seven and he is ours for life.' And they may be right.

Isn't this a contradiction of the One and Only Law? If so much is directly determined, what's the sense of constantly self-confronting anything? The sense, in a strange way, is common sense. The ability of men, women, and even children to overcome terrible odds and succeed is the history of humanity. Regardless of the '85 per cent of your luck' factor, recorded history proves that people can squeeze so much out of their potential that they can radically change their lives in momentous ways.

I wish I could tell you that all winners have the same attitude or non-attitude towards luck. That would be easy. But that is not my experience or belief. Some are superstitious, others are not. Some gamble notoriously, others wouldn't consider taking the smallest chance. I believe that those who do believe in their luck have one belief in common with those who don't: they both don't trust it.

Let me explain why.

If you go to your doctor with a minor ailment, and he nods sagely that he could cure it, you would smile. If he continues and says that you will lose no time from work, that it will cost you nothing, that you will feel no pain, you will be overjoyed. But then if he adds, 'There's only one down side to this treatment; 9999 out of every 10,000 people who take this procedure die, but the one who survives, he or she feels great.'

How would you feel? Wouldn't you be outraged? Would you confront him with his nerve, his absolute gall to suggest a treatment that would mean almost certain death for a minor ailment? And if you did confront him, and he reiterated, 'No, death isn't certain, because one in 10,000 is completely cured', would you feel any better?

Imagine the following scenario:

You leave that crazy doctor's office, saying you will stop seeing that doctor forever and you meet a friend for lunch in a nearby restaurant. You tell the friend your doctor story and you both agree he should lose his licence to practise medicine. You even decide to write to the authorities the next day. As you leave the restaurant, you see a £100,000 prize draw sponsored by a big food manufacturer and you buy a ticket. If you win you'll have a bundle of money, and you fantasise how you'll spend this newfound wealth in wonderful ways. It takes your mind off the doctor's earlier outrageous recommendation.

In the paragraph above, you read of two potential fantasies: one of defying the odds and living through a dangerous operation and one of defying the odds and winning a lot of money. Those two fantasies have one very important common denominator: *The odds of both happening are about the same, one in 10,000.* Yet the fantasy of living through a dangerous operation wasn't even considered, only the down side of it was – the probability of death. The other fantasy of winning a lot of money was freely wallowed in. Understanding why this happens when both probabilities are driven by a similar chance of occurring is important.

Fear of loss of what people already have, especially health or wealth, is a greater concern to people than promise of gain of what they might get. That is why the absolute glitter and glamour of gambling casinos (purveyors of benefit of gain), as large as successful as they are, do not have the financial substance and resources of insurance companies and banks (purveyors of fear of loss).

Go back to the scenario I just described and change the odds radically. If the medical treatment's odds were reversed, if only one in 10,000 die and 9999 live, and if the ailment was really bothersome to you, you would probably consider the treatment. But you would weigh your decision gravely. On the other hand, if the odds of winning the prize draw were increased a thousandfold, to one in 10 million, would it change the fantasy of what you would do with the money won? Not in the slightest. The party in your mind would have just as much champagne.

With the fear of loss, the odds of success are more than just important. The odds or the danger is critical to everyone.

With the promise of gain, the odds or the probability of succeeding are meaningless. People just don't care. Let me rephrase that: most people don't care. Winners do. That's one of the principal reasons they're winners.

Fear of loss is a concept that goes far beyond insurance and banking as products and services. We have all come to learn that there is more to lose in life than health and money. There is status, and we offset the fear of losing our status with the obvious symbols, from homes and vacations to the latest gadgets and the most prestigious credit cards. There is the personal acceptance of our image by others, and we protect the fear of diminishing our image with everything from clothing styles to the cars we drive. In summary, anything we have or gain, we want to keep – and keep others aware that we have it. The only problem is that the more we have, the more we have to defend, and the defence itself can take more and more time.

Promise-of-gain products go far beyond prize draws and other types of gambling. But the essential importance of gambling cannot be denied. In the United States lotteries and legal gambling take in $200 billion every year. In the nineteenth century an Italian statesman called lotteries 'a tax on imbeciles', and the statement is just as true today. But anything I or anyone else writes about the outrageous odds against winning doesn't matter.

Promise-of-gain products can sometimes be fear-of-loss products at the same time, such as anti-ageing creams. Sometimes they start as one – say, a perfume that 'drives men wild'. A woman finds she did drive at least one man wild, and she won't use anything else – so it becomes a fear-of-loss product. If it doesn't work, there'll be another perfume, another promise. No big deal.

Dare I forget how-to books, especially how-to-be successful/ winner books? These, along with the many forms of gambling, are truly the ultimate promise-of-gain products. And they are, for the most part, treated like every other bet, a quickly disposable product. If you win, you win; if you don't, no big deal, you'll try another. There are some who will read this book like that, looking for a magic solution to appear, not a law to be obeyed.

Winners do calculate the odds very thoroughly on fear-of-loss *and* promise-of-gain decisions, for they don't want to waste their money, their time . . . or their dreams. More than anything, winners know that there is with gambling a loss that goes far beyond the bet itself. To gamble is to participate in a dream you can enjoy – whether or not you win anything. You can for a time really get into the fantasy. But it's a dream you can in no way control or confront, for you must abdicate responsibility.

To understand that the odds are stacked against the gambler – and always will be – is a given. A lot of people who are not winners know and understand that. But they still take the gamble because in their eyes it's their only ticket to a better or different life.

Not so with winners. Their main focus is on what they can control and, if not control, at least confront and be responsible for. Those who do gamble don't really trust their luck, because they know it's too elusive. They understand that the playing also has to be the fantasy, and in effect the real pay-off.

An old cliché by Canadian economist/humorist Stephen Leacock, 'The harder I work the luckier I get', is certainly true, but it is incomplete. Luck is all around us all the time. It has already had an enormous effect on you and will continue to influence the story of your life. It can and will contribute to tragedy and success and there's not a lot you can do about it – except work through it.

The essential confrontation for you is not whether you believe in luck or believe yourself to be a lucky person. That is unimportant. What is important is that you don't trust your luck, good or bad, that you pursue what you must pursue to win, regardless of your luck – simply because trusting your luck is abdicating the responsibility of making your own life happen. It's that simple.

In researching this book I unexpectedly came across this appropriate thought by Mario Puzo, author of *The Godfather*.

'Luck and strength go together. When you get lucky you have to have the strength to follow through. You also have to have the strength to wait for the luck.'[1]

Perhaps I should consider myself lucky to have found that.

Note

1. *Time*, 28 August 1978.

> *Only constant self-confrontation of*
> *responsibility reaps results*

Luck and You:

Essential Self-Confrontations

- Winners, whether they believe in luck or not, do not trust luck. Do you?

- Winners acknowledge the importance of chance, but believe that they have no chance but to work through their bad luck. Do you?

- Winners who gamble know that the odds of winning are so stacked against the player that the playing must also be the pay-off. To believe otherwise would be to abdicate personal responsibility for winning. Do you share this belief?

CHAPTER 6

Winning and Confidence

Is confidence king? Is belief in yourself, self-confidence, a critical key to enforcing the One and Only Law? Some believe it is, and others even believe it is the critical key to winning.

You will be hard-pressed to find many how-to books that don't try to pump you up with the importance of 'confidence', in 'believing-in-yourself-and-your-dreams'. One goes so far as to say that everyone should be 'the master of his fate, the captain of his soul'.[1] What wonderful cadence of self-conviction! What a simple solution to the problems of life!

But is it true?

I feel that these believe-in-yourself enthusiasts of success miss two essential points. The first is that confidence cannot be put on like a coat for the world to see. It just doesn't work that way for the average person. You can't put on what doesn't fit. The second is that confidence is also not a blanket of belief that covers you like armour till the big pay-off. Rather, confidence is a daily exercise of your self-worth that creates small pay-offs every day.

To prove these points, let me give you two true-life examples that I have witnessed. One concerns the action of a man waiting for a lift; the other of a police officer immediately after making an arrest.

The man waiting for the lift was impatient. He was waiting with a group of other people, strangers, but he wasn't content to wait for the light above the lift call button to go off (which would announce that the lift was about to arrive). Pacing in front of the call button, he pressed it every seven or eight seconds and then, each time, mysteriously looked up to see if his action had helped. Of course everyone waiting knew that it hadn't. The button only had to be pressed once, and every other time was futile. This is not a rare story. We live in an impatient world. It happens all the time.

The story of the police officer is different, and rarer, but it proves the same point. Many years ago, my father owned and managed the local dance and banquet hall in the town where we lived. Every Saturday night he hired two of the town's finest to provide security for the teenage disco. One Saturday night, after a fight broke out at the end of the disco, I assisted one of the police officers in handcuffing a resistant combatant in the lobby. The policeman immediately pulled his suspect over to the pay phone, put in a coin and dialled the police station for a patrol car. I told him to forget the phone, that it was out of order, and since the office phone didn't make outgoing calls I would go to the bowling alley next door to phone the police station.

When I came back five minutes later the policeman was holding his suspect with one arm, and was putting his money in the phone with his other hand, not receiving a dial tone, hanging up, and starting over. In front of him, a group of the suspect's friends were becoming vocally angry at this scene and threatening violence. I, then, at the age of 18, made my first demonstration of leadership as an adult. I told the policeman to take his suspect into the kitchen and wait. And that's exactly what he did.

I have never forgotten that incident because, until then, I didn't think it was possible for someone with the skill and training of a police officer to panic into repeating a futile action during a crisis. I have since learned that many, many people can, and often do live a good part of their lives repeating futile actions because they have a lack of confidence in themselves.

> *Confidence is believing that you are worthy of being who you are, of what you do, what you've obtained, and that you'll be just as worthy where you're going in the future because you'll have the courage to forgive yourself for, and then learn from, all the mistakes you're going to make getting there.*

A few years ago, I was preparing a public-speaking seminar and was looking for the perfect sentence to explain to my audience that everyone will make mistakes at the podium, that the only thing that is important is to recover and go on. My friend and business associate Don Davies said, 'Tell them that their audiences will forgive them if they will only forgive themselves.' I did use Don's sentence in the seminar and was reminded of it when I saw the first 1988 Bush/Dukakis presidential debate.

When (then) Vice-President Bush stumbled on statistical information relating to missile types, instead of retreating into a perplexed apology, he looked up and said to a smiling and, some might say, smirking Governor Michael Dukakis, 'It's okay, it's Christmas, Michael, it's Christmas.' With that smiling admission of a mistake and assumption of forgiveness, he went back to clarify the point, and on to win a critical debate. The next day, most media commentators said that Bush made a mistake but 'recovered quickly'. He did more than that. He forgave himself, and the American people, seeing that and sensing his confidence, also forgave him and thought no more of it.

The two elements of confidence – believing in your self-worth and then acting on it with forgiveness and learning – are intricately linked and yet separate. The first confrontation I ask you to make about confidence is simply this: do you believe you are worthy of being who you are, what you've obtained, what you do, and where you're going?

Are you worthy? Really? I'm not saying that you don't have some doubts about what you'll achieve or even how you'll achieve your goals. That's to be expected. But is there a foundation of belief, in yourself as an individual, that you deserve what you want to achieve to be a winner? If you strongly doubt your self-worth, any amount of positive pumping-up with slogans of confidence will only offer temporary relief. It will be like inflating a tyre with a slash in it. The tyre will continue to deflate until the slash is repaired. So it is with confidence.

If lack of confidence is keeping you from achieving your goals, you will have to consider one of two possible areas of repair: education, which can give you the knowledge to be confident (if that's what you lack), or psychology (and I include therapy), which can give you the reason for your lack of confidence (if that's what you lack).

Think carefully and choose wisely. Without confidence you cannot win.

The second confrontation about confidence I ask you to make is easier, because it does not need the time or financial investment of the first, but still requires total honesty and introspection: do you believe that you use wisely the confidence that you now have?

I feel that many people have earned their own respect (along with the respect of others). Yes, they really believe in their own self-worth. Yet they often retreat to an earlier, less confident pattern of behaviour when things don't go right. Alas, as we all know or learn, in life things don't go right more often than they do.

Let's look at the two examples that started this chapter.

The man waiting for the lift may have had a strong concept of self-worth, but it wasn't strong enough to overcome an exaggerated nervous reaction that demonstrated a definite lack of confidence in the situation he found himself in. Maybe he had a reputation for being extremely punctual and he was on his way to the most important meeting of the year; perhaps he was going to be late for an important job interview. It doesn't matter. He couldn't forgive himself for that lift not being there, and he couldn't control his anxiety as evidenced by his repeated pushing of the call button. This hurt his chances of having anyone else forgive him.

This type of exaggerated reaction is also heard in the millions of car horns that honk needlessly in clogged city streets, in the countless arguments people have over their expectations that the other person is mistaken, and in so many other things that go wrong every day to all of us. Our most natural reaction is to return to an emotional pattern of behaviour, to react to frustration with immediate anger rather than with self-forgiveness, learning and – ultimately – confronting our own responsibility for whatever situation we find ourselves in.

The example of the police officer is different, yet just as demonstrative of a lack of confidence. The 'freeze and repeat reaction' can have serious, even life-threatening consequences in the business of law enforcement. It can also seriously hamper the success of average people who react illogically to things that have gone wrong.

How many salespeople, after being rejected by a prospect, find that they cannot forgive themselves for the feeling of rejection, much less learn from it? These types get locked into a behaviour pattern that avoids rejection and encourages them to do anything but be in a similar selling situation for a substantial amount of time. They go for long lunches, have lengthy coffee breaks with associates, do paperwork – anything to procrastinate and lick the wound slowly, rather than forgive, learn and move on to the next challenge quickly.

And you certainly don't have to be in sales to fall victim to 'freeze and repeat reaction' behaviour. Anyone who finds himself in a difficult situation and reacts with repetitive behaviour that is counter-productive to his life is demonstrating this same lack of confidence. This is true of the corporate chairman who blithely ignores a competitor's successful new product and proceeds with his old ones.

There can be no constant self-confrontation of responsibility without confidence in confronting the challenges that arise in life with action. To this end, confidence is critical to winning.

In discussing the subject of confidence with others I have almost become convinced that many people have a common and fond memory of one unusual teacher from their schooldays. Usually a woman, this teacher was quiet and never made threats. Discipline was handed out matter-of-factly, dispassionately, and consistently to anyone who broke her rules. Even the goody-goody kids who could sometimes get away with more than the badly behaved ones received equal justice in the classroom. We weren't in her class more than three days before we realised that this teacher would have the confidence and nerve to send every kid to the head's office if she had to, and teach no one, rather than teach under conditions that were counter-productive to learning. She had an awesome amount of confidence.

What is surprising is that she stands out, that we still remember her, and that her type is so few in number. What is interesting is how many or few among us have truly learned the most important lesson she taught us.

No, confidence is not just cheap bravado about mastering your destiny. It is not puffery or slogans that send you through life with armour to deflect the everyday problems that attack us all. It is knowledge of self-worth, it is self-forgiveness, it is learning, it is going on, it is confronting problems and acting with consistency in what we believe.

Confidence is critical to enforcing the One and Only Law of Winning. But please, understand what confidence really is.

Notes

1. Paraphrasing William Ernest Henley's poem, 'Invictus'.

> *Only constant self-confrontation of*
> *responsibility reaps results*

Confidence and You:

Essential Self-Confrontations

- Do you believe yourself worthy of what you've attained and what you want in life? If not, are you willing to find out why?

- Do you believe you wisely exercise the confidence you now have to confront the challenge of life with positive action?

CHAPTER 7

Winning and Justice

'The only problem with her is that she's so hard on herself.' My female luncheon guest was commenting on a mutual friend. Her eyebrows rose in a quizzical lack of understanding at the following response I gave her.

'Yes, I know,' I told my guest, 'that's one of the reasons I really like her. She's harder on herself than anyone else ever can be or ever will be.'

I then went on to explain what I meant, and that's what this chapter is about: justice. It's related to the chapters that have preceded this – what you believe about blame, failure, luck and confidence – but it's separate; it's about how you extend yourself.

According to American Supreme Court Justice Oliver Wendell Holmes, Jr, 'The life of the law has not been logic: it has been experience.' I don't believe there is a better definition of the evolution of jurisprudence than that. The One and Only Law of Winning extends this definition by saying that winners try to get ahead of their experience.

Winners learn from experience better than other people simply because the very idea of constant self-confrontation of responsibility forces us either to learn or to be aware of problems immediately. This means considering personal justice (which you can read as 'fairness') as a wonderful thing for other people. Winners hope that from time to time fairness can fall on them. But winners are not surprised when it doesn't.

Because they know life is not fair, winners are harder on themselves than anyone else ever could be or ever will be. Winners often work harder, sometimes think longer, and will sometimes endure the scorn or ridicule of others for their idiosyncratic beliefs or behaviour.

Sometimes this is just because that is the way they are. Often it's because they want to get ahead of their experience. They want to see around a corner before they get to the corner. They want to risk and maybe even waste their own time because they know time is a non-refundable and non-returnable asset that costs nothing yet can be spent freely by those who are motivated to get ahead in life.

This is not a matter of attitude. Optimists and pessimists alike share this trait in enforcing the One and Only Law (on themselves). This is a matter of character. This is a matter of carving out a personal code of behaviour and work habits when the accepted code – what they can easily get away with – is much less.

Can winners take this too far? Of course. As soon as they start applying their personal code to others who do not share it, conflict does ensue. So they must learn not to expect of others what they expect of themselves.

> *Only constant self-confrontation of*
> *responsibility reaps results*

Justice and You:

Essential Self-Confrontations

- Do you believe that life should be fair but acknowledge that it probably won't be for you?

- Do you believe you get ahead of your experience by working harder or longer for what you want?

- Are you harder on yourself than anyone else could be?

CHAPTER 8

Winning and Trust

You probably realise by now that I have, at least in my head, been writing this book for years – designing its format, weighing its components, recalling and digging up references. One belief I saw as being critical to the One and Only Law, but which escaped my analysis, was the concept of trust. I felt it was important. But where? Here, in asking you to confront what you believe? Or later, in another section of the book?

And was trust really that important? Where was the common bond among winners with the concept of trust? If anything, winners seem to vary greatly in the degree of trust they relay to others. There are many examples of people – especially business people – who build empires by hiring people who are smarter than they and trusting them implicitly. Then there are others who seem to control every detail that touches their success and limit trust in every way.

Initial research made me wonder whether I shouldn't drop the subject. There was, it seemed, a lot less trust in the world in recent years. There was the 'credibility gap' with government and politicians, the unreliability of products, the breakdown in service, even the unreasonable suspicions of neighbours. But what about personal trust? That's what I was really after.

An article published in *Psychology Today* entitled 'Trust and Gullibility' moved me closer to where I wanted to be. It demonstrated documented proof (in case the reader doesn't trust the author) that those who are 'high trusters' – that is, who trust more than others – are 'more trustworthy', 'more likeable', in the opinion of both high and low trusters alike. And this was important: 'They are not more gullible.'[1]

While the information was comforting, I didn't initially see how it could be self-confrontational in nature. I kept wondering if there was an essential truth to be believed, and really to be confronted by everyone.

I wasn't really sure I could apply this information to winning so my research dug deeper.

'Trust as a Social Reality' was a scientific paper published in the sociological journal *Social Forces*.[2] Unfortunately, its authors didn't use popular jargon or easy language for non-scientific readers such as myself. Let me give you just the first two sentences from the abstract of this paper:

> Although trust is an underdeveloped concept in sociology, promising theoretical formulations are available. . . . These sociological versions complement the psychological and attitudinal conceptualizations of experimental and survey researchers.

Okay, you get the picture. I confess I have a problem with reading scientific papers, one I believe I share with many others. I liken it to my ability to learn dance steps. I can learn them, but forget them ten minutes later. In reading scientific papers, if I really concentrate, and have some knowledge and interest in the subject, I can burrow my way through, but as soon as I turn a page I have a hard time recalling what was on the previous one.

That's the way I read 'Trust as a Social Reality', and I was concerned enough about my ability to understand that I made a point of reading the entire paper twice. And I'm very glad I did, because I missed the essential confrontation I was looking for the first time. There, on the ninth page of this article, were five words that started a paragraph: 'Trust begins where prediction ends.'

Those five words, dear reader, are why you are reading about trust here, and why I am going to ask you to confront what you believe on the subject.

To those five words, 'Trust begins where prediction ends', I found myself adding, 'and stops where experience directs.'

Trust and mistrust (often called 'precaution') are used by everyone all the time. Some examples of precaution are:

- No one leaves the door to his home unlocked at night just

64

because the majority of people are not burglars.

- We might carry around an umbrella even though the weather forecast only calls for a 30 per cent chance of rain.

On a day-to-day basis, who and what we trust move into the realm of what we believe to be common sense.

However, when we look into the very specific picture of winning and losing, the concept of trust and how we use it is critical in two aspects of life, both of which have determining effects on winning: *control* and *judgement*.

Control

'Trust begins where prediction ends' are the truest words I've ever seen to describe how each of us attempts to seek control of our lives by either expanding or containing trust. Our use of trust relates to the expectations and dreams each of us has for our future. As I see it, each of us carries one of two distinct pictures in the creative part of our minds, a 'contained image' or an 'expandable image'.

Contained image

There is no better example of the contained image than the person of exceptional talent – the painter, writer, sculptor, or athlete – who seeks the personal perfection of a vision he or she 'sees'. These do-it-yourself types of people may relay little or no trust to others simply because prediction does not end in their work. What they 'see' is a prediction of what they will create, and the contribution of others may only get in the way.

Of the composer Andrew Lloyd Webber, *Time* magazine reported:

> On the most basic level there is his insistence on dominating everything related to his music. With a nose for business as keen as his faculty for churning out hits, Lloyd Webber keeps the reins of power tightly in his hand.[3]

Expandable image

The expandable image is the vision most people carry simply because they cannot predict the limits of their lives, especially in their work. There is no better example than the business entrepreneur. His or her ideas may be very creative indeed, but they can only be fulfilled by the participation of others.

Chris Whittle is considered the American boy wonder of communication. His company, Whittle Communications, has created exceptionally successful magazines, newsletters, videos, wall media, and a syndicated radio programme. And Whittle's style of management is very high on trust. *Advertising Age* reported:

> Whittle is based on six free-floating divisions. The divisions don't have formal names; they're listed on company financial statements according to their president's name, such as Finn's Division, for division president Peter Finn.[4]

Talk about trust! Can you imagine Marks and Spencer changing its division names to those of its management heads? But Whittle has a reason for doing this which he shared with *Advertising Age* readers: 'You care a lot more about performance if your name is on the division', he said. 'That personalises performance.'

You don't have to be a show business impresario like Lloyd Webber or a communications entrepreneur like Whittle to understand that the work you do is directly related to the trust you extend to others. With very little extension of trust, you must obviously do more yourself. In business there is no better (or more frustrating) example of conflict of trust than the person in sales with a contained vision who sells exceptionally well (knowing what or 'seeing' what the client needs) but does nothing to extend trust via communication to the production and administration people who must fill his or her orders. Acting as a lone wolf can get the sale, but it is the pack which must produce, and very often salespeople must be part of the pack – the producing team – for the company as a whole to maximise its success. There are exceptions of course, and it is the wise salesperson with a contained vision who learns to change his or her ways to trusting the team or seeks employment in an environment where trusting relationships are not critical.

We'll come back to this.

Judgement

As important as trust is in the area of control, it is just as important, I believe, in the area of judgement. Trust begins where prediction ends, and stops where experience directs. Experience directs us to judgement – about people and events. And the judgements we make have a very direct bearing on our ability to win. As the cliché says, 'Experience is the best teacher', but experience that involves misuse of trust is often a very poor teacher, because it can encourage dropping out of the very process of winning.

I believe a great many people either overlearn or underlearn from seeing their trust abused. Very few learn how to confront themselves and their trust accurately.

The underlearners are the gullible who believe in the golden promises of others, rush to participate, are shattered, and wait for the next person to come along and then repeat the process. An example is the person who tends to make friends with particular type, sees his or her trust shattered, and then finds someone very similar to repeat the experience with. It seems that underlearners just won't admit to a flaw in their judgement, won't allow for the fact that they can be wrong, and don't take corrective action by confronting their trust itself. They are forever opening themselves up for certain defeat by not learning from their past mistakes.

Just as self-damaging are the overlearners, who will pronounce a judgement on a person, or even on an idea that fails their trust, with more severity than can ever be warranted. 'I tried that once and it didn't work' is a typical phrase from an overlearner. From that one experience a categorical judgement sweeps their mind and heavily influences their entire life. To these people trust is the most fragile commodity in their world, and betrayal, or seeming betrayal, of their trust is a crushing experience with lifelong consequences. From the lover who cheats on them to the garage mechanic who rips them off, everyone is suspected and never quite trusted because of this perception.

This is where acquired prejudice is formed, ambitions are unfulfilled and lives are narrowed.

It can be difficult to trust, to transfer to someone else a power over your life that you cannot predict, cannot control, not even influence. But we all must trust to one degree or another, in order to survive and prosper, simply because so many of the events in our lives are unpredictable.

We must also make judgements, not only about those who abuse our trust but about our trust itself when it has been shattered. We have to ask, 'What have I learned in order to change whom or what I trust?' This is precision learning that winners acquire.

The first confrontation I ask of you is to consider what you believe about the very nature of your trust. In the area of your work, which do you have, a contained trust or an expandable trust? Or both? More importantly, which do you need?

The second confrontation concerns what you believe about trust in other relationships with people. Do you judge your trust as accurately as you judge people? Do you tend to underlearn, overlearn, or learn with precision when your trust is abused?

These are difficult questions to answer, I know, and, because of the importance of the subject, I am challenging you to confront yourself on the answers. *Trust begins where prediction ends and stops where experience directs.*

The correct prediction and the right direction contribute significantly to winning.

Notes

1. *Psychology Today*, October 1980.
2. *Social Forces*, June 1985.
3. *Time*, 18 January 1988.
4. *Advertising Age*, 16 May 1988.

Only constant self-confrontation of
responsibility reaps results

Trust and You:

Essential Self-Confrontations

- Do you believe you employ a contained or an expandable vision of trust, and have you considered if it's right for your life and work?

- Do you believe you accurately judge the nature of your trust, and whether you either overlearn or underlearn from life experiences?

CHAPTER 9

Winning and Risk

There is no person more honoured, respected, or rewarded in business than the risk taker. He or she seems to be everywhere important – courted by the powerful, the recipient of honorary degrees, in the middle of the media spotlight. There is only one condition necessary for the risk taker to receive these honours, respect, and rewards: success.

To some, risk taking is gambling, plain and simple, and they will have no part of it. To others, risk taking is life, the best reason to get up in the morning. Whether the reason for this disparity of belief (and everything in between) is biological or environmental is not important. What is important for you is to understand that all winners do take risks, but that the degrees of risk do vary greatly and that greater success does not necessarily come with greater risk. Furthermore, you must know the type of risk you are willing and able to take in order to achieve what you want.

There are, broadly speaking, four kinds of risk you can take: impulsive, cherished, visualised and calculated.

Impulsive risk

This is the only type I consider to be the 100 per cent gamble – because of its very nature. Out of the blue, with such speed that the risk taker surprises him or herself, there is an impulsive grab for something without rational examination of the potential success, the cost or the circumstances. The person who takes the impulsive risk typically keeps money in a bank for security only and then, suddenly, on the basis of a tip, risks all of it on a roller-coaster stock or investment. This is the person who goes shopping for a compact car and suddenly buys the big, glossy saloon car at twice the intended price and now risks not being able to make the payments.

Every impulsive risk has this common feature. The risk itself is usually hated but the object of desire is very much wanted.

Cherished risk

This is just the opposite of an impulsive risk, not in being any more rational, but in the maturity of the desire. This is when someone pursues a wish he or she has had for a long time, 'You know, I've always dreamed of . . .'. This risk taker is the person who trades a secure career for an interest that has always been a passion but never a commitment of time. This is someone who wants to buy something special, not that he or she needs it – it could be a rare piece of art or even a football team – but because he or she simply wants it. More than anything, this is a trade: job security for personal interest, money for a possession. The risk is in not knowing whether it will be worth it, whether after finally achieving the desire, the risk taker might want to turn the clock back and not have it.

Visualised risk

This type of risk might be cherished and it might not. For this risk taker, something will exist in the future that he or she can 'see' clearly today. It might be an invention, a new work of art, an idea for a new product or a new company. This certainly springs from the contained image of trust detailed in the last chapter. To pursue this risk takes guts and determination, because no one else 'sees' or understands exactly the way the visionary risk taker does.

Dr Raymond Domadian, the inventor of magnetic resonance scanners used for cancer and other diseases, was scorned for his vision. According to an article in *US News and World Report*:

. . . prestigious scientific journals refused to publish his findings, and government funding bodies refused to support his research. . . . At one point the chairman of his [university] department disconnected his telephones and threatened to kick him out of the lab.[1]

All because of his persistence in exploring a vision.

Dr Domadian did persist, did prove he was right, and today he is the president of the company he set up to manufacture his scanners. What kept him going? He is quoted in the same article: 'The concept was extremely clear in my head – down to the finest minutiae.'

Calculated risk

This is the risk most used by most people, and most organisations. This is the risk that is taken with a keen eye on the down-side, usually with a plan for escape if failure results. The calculated risk may be as fraught with danger as any other kind, but the risk, one way or another, is hedged. An example is the person who wants to take the cherished risk of leaving a secure job for a passionate interest, but instead of leaving immediately, takes unpaid leave of absence just to be sure.

In business there is no better example of a calculated risk taker than Richard Branson, head of the UK Virgin Group plc. Known for his expertise in running a record company, Branson surprised many when he started Virgin Atlantic, an airline that flies Boeing 747s from Britain to the United States and continental Europe on a low fare/full service basis. The *Toronto Globe and Mail* stated in a profile of him:

> Mr Branson also sticks to his business credo, protect the down-side. . . . He negotiated a deal with Boeing Co of Seattle that would allow him to return his jets after the first, second or third year, just in case the airline business didn't fly.[2]

As a personal level of understanding of the calculated risk, I believe Sylvester Stallone provides an excellent example. An unknown actor and writer, he brought his *Rocky* script to producers as a package, with himself playing the lead. Needless to say, producers, although enthralled with the script, didn't really want Stallone in the lead. He admits:

> Now the point was, was I marketable? Of course not. Nobody knew me outside of close relations and enemies. But I couldn't sell out. They were offering me $265,000 and 5 per cent of the gross. But I was more desperate than hungry. If I had sold out, I could see myself getting angry and slapping my wife around and losing myself in a bottle of Four Roses. I knew how I wanted that part acted, so I decided to sell the script only if I went with the deal. The worst that could happen would be that I would be rejected. I would not be shot, I would not be drawn and quartered, I would just go back to Encino.[3]

The essential point was that Stallone had thought through the risk completely and was prepared for the down-side. Even if *Rocky* had never been made, that essential confrontation with himself provided a definition of his responsibility to his own success. He was on his way, regardless.

It would be too easy to say the calculated risk is the only risk to follow because it offers a parachute in the sense of an optional plan for the down-side: failure. It certainly is the most practical. But people, their dreams and opportunities, do not always coincide in a practical manner or at a practical time. There is no certain formula.

The confrontation I ask of you here is this: do you have the cold-blooded tenacity to confront yourself in terms of your capacity for risk, for what you can accept and what you can't, and in terms of your ambitions, for what you want? How many business ventures, partnerships, new jobs, and various relationships result in failure because there is a profound belief in a visualised risk with a healthy dose of calculation, only to find the vision wasn't real and the calculations were woefully inadequate or unacceptable?

This chapter is not intended to stunt or obstruct your dreams. It will, I hope, encourage them, for I believe a dream has a better chance of not being shattered if the risk it requires is better understood and confronted before it is taken. And if the dream is shattered, no one picks the pieces up like a winner because, often, that's what winning is all about.

Notes

1. *U.S. News and World Report*, 26 January 1987.
2. *Toronto Globe and Mail*, 9 May 1988.
3. *Writer's Digest*, July 1977.

> *Only constant self-confrontation of*
> *responsibility reaps results*

Risk and You:

The Essential Self-Confrontation

- Winners can take four kinds of risk. Do you believe you have
  the capacity for the type of risk you require in order to acquire
  what you want?

Part 3

Practising the Law

Habits are investments, the biggest investments we make with our time. They are the repetitive and reactionary actions of our lives and they either pay us dividends or squander our potential.

The One and Only Law of Winning forces you to confront your habits: what you do, day in and day out. As you practise the law, you also enforce it. That is what the following seven chapters are all about.

CHAPTER 10

Strength: Find it and Use it

Let me now tell you a personal story of a search for strength. It starts with a weakness that first appears to be the cause of a failure, is next seen as an obscenity, and then as an agony. Later, it causes a mistake that identifies a strength – and launches a career.

In 1962, I first ran into the very hard wall of unexpected failure. A very skinny and intense teenager, I went to work as a teller for a trust company the day after my final school examination. I might go to a university later, I reasoned, but I wanted the experience of working and paying my own way in a giant world I saw before me.

Within two weeks, I learned of another good reason for not applying to university. My examination results were sent to my home and revealed that I would not be receiving my diploma because I had failed one subject, English literature, which I normally breezed through. It was a 'departmental' examination; that is, it was taken by everyone in the last year of school, at the same time, on the same day, and marked anonymously at a central location by a teacher who didn't know the person whose exam paper was being marked. And I had failed.

I appealed against the mark, but it came back the same. In my heart I knew why. It didn't concern the content of my answers but the style. My handwriting, atrocious at best, had been stretched beyond comprehension by the long, detailed answers I had provided. Every year in school I had gone out of my way to 'teach' my teachers the meaning of my scrawls. And then an anonymous teacher failed me because he or she could not read my handwriting.

Less than a year later, I was harmed once more by the same weakness. The trust company's internal auditors paid our branch a visit and within two days of their arrival I was summoned into the manager's office for a solemn meeting with the manager and two auditors.

Why me? I wondered. I had done nothing wrong. What did they want? I was innocent. But I was more than scared – I was petrified.

'Bern, the auditors have discovered a very serious problem that concerns you,' the manager stated with the gravity of a judge about to pass sentence on a major criminal.

I said nothing. I didn't have to. I don't think I was shaking visibly, but my eyes were open so wide it would have taken me ten seconds to blink.

'The problem,' said the senior auditor, 'concerns customer ledger cards.'

I then saw that he had a pile of ledger cards on the side of the manager's desk. This was probably the last branch of the last trust company or bank in the West to automate ledger cards. We still had to complete all deposits and withdrawals by hand on the ledger cards and duplicate every transaction in the customer's passbook.

The senior auditor was tapping the pile of cards and perhaps waiting for me to blink before he went on, but he gave up. 'When you complete a card and have another entry, what do you do?' he asked.

'I forward the balance to a new card,' I answered earnestly.

'How do you do that?'

Was this a trap? He had a pile of cards in front of him and I could see that the top one had my forwarding scrawl across it.

'I write the date, the number of the new card, the balance in the account, and the word forward.'

'"Forward"? How do you spell that?'

'I use the short form, like everyone else: fwd.'

'Like this?' he said, holding up a card for me to see.

'Yes, like that,' I replied.

'Young man, these letters are not f, w, and d. They are f, u, c, and k!'

My eyeballs didn't have time to consider the relief of blinking. They were too busy rotating into the interior of my brain.

The junior auditor, silent until now, walked over and picked up the ledger cards on the desk. He wore the scowl of a man who looked like this entire process was beneath his dignity. 'And we have here,' he said, 'more than a hundred of these cards, legal company documents, with this obscenity written all over them.'

'They say "forward",' I yelled, 'fwd! I do not write obscenities.' I had more than a tinge of anger in my voice and my eyes were probably popping.

The manager intervened. 'Okay, Bern, we just want to make sure that this was an accident, that you weren't purposely. . . . You can go now.'

The next day, the manager took me aside to say that I was a good kid but that perhaps the banking world wasn't necessarily my best choice for a career and that I should consider looking for another line of work.

I did take my manager's advice but, as you will see, I was on a learning curve that was inverted.

A year and a half later, I found myself working as a statistician in the head office of a major shoe corporation. One of my duties was preparing handwritten transparencies of financial performance for executives to view on a screen. (This was just before computers took over this function.) The problem, beyond the questionable legibility of my handwriting, was the fact that being left-handed, and writing from left to right, my hand when hurried, smeared the wet ink as fast as I could write the numbers. After one of the executives complained to the head statistician that he had 'seen profit drop before but never with such agony' as I had provided, my boss had a talk with me. It was all very similar to my talk with the branch manager of the trust company. I was a good guy, but maybe I should consider looking for work in another field.

So when did I start to learn? It took a couple more years. By that time I was writing short stories – none of them published – and I decided to apply for a job in advertising. At the time, I was working as a clerk in an oil company and had the task of calculating the amount of oil left in the tanks at the end of the day. This time, I could actually see the computer program being written to replace this function and I also knew I had less of an affinity with computers than I did with competent penmanship.

A classified ad I answered for the position of junior writer in the advertising department of an insurance company resulted in an interview with an administrator, and that led to an interview with the marketing officer who would make the hiring decision. I hit it off immediately with the marketing officer. Just as the interview was finishing, when we were deciding the best day for me to start my new job, he glanced down at the handwritten letter that had accompanied my résumé and asked, 'Just how many of the short stories you've written have been published?'

'Published?' I queried.

'Yes, we had a lot of applications for this job, but the reason I wanted to see you was that you say here' – he was now looking intently at my letter – 'that some of your short stories have been published.'

I peered over his desk at my letter and put my forefinger on the misinterpreted letters. 'No, that's not an s,' I said sincerely and honestly. 'It's an n. And that's not an m, it's an n. None of my short stories have been published.'

He studied the letter for a moment and even squinted his eyes at my twisted handwriting. Then he laughed. 'Can you start in two weeks?'

That I did, and for more than 20 years in advertising and related businesses I have not looked back. Every day I go to work to do work I love to do.

Do you?

I know that everyone has a different attitude to the subject of work. Everyone enjoys work to different degrees. Some will never enjoy any kind of work and others will enjoy work to the exclusion of everything else in life.

Should you look for something in between, a happy medium? I'm not saying that what you do for a living has to be everything in your life, but I make this three-point observation about winners: We carry the conviction that we are very good at what we do, we enjoy our work and often immerse ourselves in it to stay on top. Conviction, enjoyment, and immersion.

Please note that I do not believe you have to be a workaholic. Your work doesn't have to be the only passion in your life in order for you to be a winner, but it has to be one of them.

Winners act from strength, not weakness, and the fact is that no one is good at everything. And compensating for weakness does not create strength. I could have gone to classes until I was qualified to practise calligraphy and it wouldn't have made me a better banker. The strong administrative skills required for banking are not – and never will be – a part of me, and I would still be floundering in weakness if I had (miraculously) remained there. My handwriting was as much a symptom of the problem as the problem itself. (I now have an administrative assistant who is extremely talented at reading poor handwriting.)

So far you've read that the law does expect you to take responsibility, actually confront it, work without luck, banish blame, analyse failure, calculate risks, hone your concept of trust and be tougher on yourself than anyone else could ever be. BUT IT DOES NOT EXPECT YOU TO BANG YOUR HEAD AGAINST THE WALL OF THE IMPOSSIBLE. For some people, the type of work they are doing will be that wall. If all three elements – conviction, enjoyment, and immersion – are not there, they will be in trouble.

There are three important confrontations here: deciding whether you face that wall, doing something about it if you do, and possibly improving on your strength in your present work if you don't. All are important for consideration.

When you think about it, it is actually surprising that so many people are so well suited to their work. Somewhere between the ages of 16 and 24 – the most confusing and erratic time of life for a lot of us (certainly me, and probably you) – we are supposed to choose a career that will take us, health willing, over almost half a century. Talk about luck. Somehow, most people seem to succeed. Sometimes it's an inner direction. Sometimes it's not. As roundabout as my stumbling entrance into advertising was, with the weakness of my handwriting working *for* me to land an important interview, it was not all that rare. More people have 'fallen into' careers that are perfect for them than I would ever have believed possible.

A chance meeting . . . an intriguing magazine article . . . talking to someone at a party . . . and dozens of other haphazard events have led to something that led to new and often different careers. One of my favourite stories comes from a man who was my neighbour and a professor of business administration.

After his last year of school he was convinced that he should become an engineer and lined up in the registrar's office for engineer admissions only to find at the end of his long wait he was in the wrong line, the line for business school. He said to himself, 'I'm here anyway,' and, knowing he could always change later, decided to give business school a try. He became hooked on business, and is today, in my opinion, a quintessential business professor.

Yes, you can 'fall' and win, and you can also 'fall' and lose.

It is tragic that there are many people who have no inner direction and don't 'fall into' the right career – business, trade or profession. The percentage of people in the wrong career varies according to whom you ask. I've seen it as high as 50 per cent for business people and 30 per cent for people in general. I believe a truer figure is somewhere in the 20–25 per cent range. That means that one out of four or five people do not enjoy their work, have limited or no conviction of their value to it, and have no desire to immerse themselves in it. Ever. So bitterness, the blood brother of blame, sets in. And you already know where that leads.

The One and Only Law of Winning is a tough enough law to practise without having also to fight yourself. If you are one of those people in the wrong career, you should evaluate your circumstances and change them; otherwise you certainly cannot win.

In my years, I have seen tough corporate managers sink in the cultural seas of big businesses because they didn't have the interpersonal and political skills necessary to survive. They were hard-working, hard-driven, and entrepreneurial managers who should have been in their own business or at least a small business. There was something in their nature that didn't let them exploit the potential of their corporate environment. I've also seen salespeople disguised as housewives, clerks and factory workers, and the disguises are indeed unfortunate for so much potential is lost. And I've seen various missionaries who have lost the zeal for their missions and truly creative people who have no mission for their zeal. They're especially lost.

I can accurately say these things for one out of every four or five people I know. So can you. The question, the real question, is this: Can you definitely say any of these things about yourself?

84

It is important not to answer this question too quickly. Business psychologist Srully Blotnick wrote in *Forbes* magazine: '70 % of those who make a career change will make another within five years.'[1] That's a serious number and it represents, to me, people who are not changing careers wisely but rather, are moving away from the reality of responsibility. In all probability, people who change careers twice in five years are further away from the law than they were before they began changing careers.

You should be wary of making a career change for the wrong reason. Just because you don't like your boss, or because your job has unusual frustrations, or because you have to work overtime does not mean you should immediately start looking for a new job. On the other hand, you could encounter none of these and find yourself lacking in the three critical areas of conviction, enjoyment, and immersion.

In the coming chapters, you will see how once you are acting from strength, you can maximise additional aspects of your life and work. Here are four options for you to consider.

Action from strength: four options

1: Develop a complementary focus to your work

For some, this will be an easy option because it sounds too simple, yet it can be vital for understanding and appreciating the strengths you are using every day. Before considering a career change, consider doing something outside work that you'd really like to do as an extra interest.

If you really want to be a singer, join a choir, a rock group, a barber-shop quartet. If you want to work with animals, volunteer to work at your local animal refuge. There are few interests that don't have available night classes. I know an accountant who recently became a part-time actor in a little theatre; I know he is now a better accountant because he's no longer a frustrated actor. He does both, but there is no doubt that it's his accounting practice that pays the bills.

For a lot of people, developing another outside interest is really necessary in order for them to see the strength they do bring to their work. An interesting side benefit of this is that the outside interest just may lead to an entirely new career. Try it. If you find that you're still spinning your wheels, then read on.

2: Sharpen the focus where you are

You may be inches, not miles, from acting from strength but you might not know it. Where you're working right now might be the perfect place to keep working – but with a different focus. Dow Jones and Co pioneered what they call the 'Druthers Programme'.[2] Employees are encouraged to look for new jobs within the company by writing a 'Druthers Letter' that begins, 'If I had my druthers . . .' to the department he or she prefers to change to.

Even if your organisation has no formal intra-company employment programme, it is possible to focus on an area in which you want to work and make a presentation to the department or person you'd like to be working for. In one of my early advertising jobs I found myself working for the advertising manager when the research manager was really responsible for an area I wanted to work in. I spoke to both managers, pointed out my strengths and the opportunity that I perceived to be at hand, and convinced them to let me make the switch. In his *Forbes* article, Srully Blotnick presented a lawyer who felt he made a mistake in not going into investment banking but had no desire to go back to school. Blotnick's solution for the lawyer: switch to specialising in securities law in order to be closer to his interest.

Your solution may not require anything as dramatic as any of these examples. Perhaps a small change in your job description will let you pursue an interest that matches an opportunity you perceive or solve some problem for your employer. Don't be afraid to ask. Maybe all it will take is a heart-to-heart talk with your boss on how you can contribute more by focusing more on your strengths. This is such a simple option that it is often overlooked by the more radical options that follow.

3: Change employers

Changing to a different job in your present career path that will let you act from your strength is a drastic, but sometimes necessary, step. Every employer is different and for your unique strengths to be fully used, it may be necessary to make this kind of change. But only after exhausting your other options. That said, much of what is advised in the next option could very well apply to you.

4: Completely change your career

This is scary for most people because it shakes the very roots of their lives, their identities having become linked to their work. This means throwing in the towel on a career you once thought was perfect for you (and maybe it once was). This means giving up on the comforts and the habits you are acquainted with. (You will develop new ones in your new surroundings.) This means abandoning the friends and relationships you've nurtured over the years at work. (Being too comfortable with your colleagues and routine does not always challenge you to perform your very best.)

What are your strengths? How can you know for sure what change will be perfect for you? I don't believe there is any way to know for certain. But there certainly is help available, if you have to make this change.

First and foremost, read everything there is to read on the subject of career changing. And I mean everything. Spend days or weeks on it. Next, call on people already in the field that you're interested in joining and ask them about what strengths are necessary. You will be surprised to find out how helpful people can be when they realise you need advice on something that they are expert on: their own job or business. I was buying shoes recently when a man came in and asked the manager if the shop was a franchise. (It wasn't.) He then went on to tell the manager that he had already talked to three dozen franchise shoeshop owners but he wanted to talk to a lot more before he decided whether to get into the shoe business or not. He ended up talking a long time to a total stranger about the pros and cons of being in the shoe business.

Last, and most certainly, get professional help. There is a booming industry in career consultancies and many books have been written on the subject of careers advice. Career counselling can be very worthwhile for both evaluating what you can do in your present situation to act from strength and for marketing yourself to your new field of interest. In the final analysis, you may discover that you have strengths you are not using, or not applying correctly, in your present position.

There are two more stories I have to tell you. They are from people who live in two different worlds, but, interestingly, from the point of view of acting from their strength they are like neighbours who live on the 'same street'.

Pam Postema is the only woman umpire in professional baseball in the US. During 1988 spring training she was trying to break into the major league and *Sports Illustrated* profiled her. The magazine wrote:

> . . . since graduating from umpire school in 1977 she has been spat on, sworn at, booed and propositioned by players. Her collarbone has been broken by a high fastball and her toe broken by a foul tip.[3]

The magazine went on to say that Ms Postema played down the feminist issue:

> 'I don't want to be a cause and I don't think I am one,' she revealed. 'I umpire because I love the game and because it's such a challenge. Whatever I do I like to be good at it. I like to be at the top of the pile.'

The next story is about William Black, who was profiled in the *Wall Street Journal* when he left his position on the management committee of the prestigious investment bank Morgan Stanley and Company in order to study design and architecture. Black admitted he could have amassed a 'sizeable fortune' if he'd stayed at Morgan Stanley, but he reflected,

> 'I really wanted to shift gears and engage in something I found interesting for a long time, and be able to pace it myself, control it myself, set the scale of it myself.'[4]

The work philosophies of these two motivated individuals are well worth considering. These are not 'average' examples – they're exceptional, which is why they were reported in the media. Yet the essence of both – of acting from strength, of finding conviction, enjoyment, and immersion in what they did – is a parallel trait that runs through the lives of all true winners. Without fanfare and without media interviews, typical winners find and hone their strengths every day. Playwright George Bernard Shaw once summed it up best when he said in a film interview: 'The secret of a happy life is to do work you enjoy and then you'll be too busy to know whether you're happy or not.'

There is absolutely nothing more important than acting from strength, and there is no greater self-confrontation you can make. Whatever your strength or strengths are, find them and use them. You won't be sorry if you do, and you almost certainly will be if you don't – for you won't be following the One and Only Law of Winning.

Notes

1. *Forbes*, 9 February 1987.
2. *Canadian Business*, November 1985.
3. *Sports Illustrated*, 14 March 1988.
4. *Wall Street Journal*, 6 October 1986.

> *Only constant self-confrontation of
> responsibility reaps results*

Strength and You:

Essential Self-Confrontations

- Do you find conviction, enjoyment and immersion in your work?

- If you don't, are you ready to try to improve on your strengths where you are presently working?

- If you can't improve on your strengths in your present work, are you prepared to move to another job or, possibly, another career?

CHAPTER 11

Attention: Pay the Full Price

Every year millions of pupils' end of year reports are delivered to parents and, I dare say, more than a few million of them contain, in similar language, the following message:

> . . . is a very bright and able student but performing much below her ability due to severe inattentiveness. If she would learn to pay attention, to concentrate on tasks at hand, her results would improve immensely.

I'm almost surprised that teachers haven't taken to making rubber stamps to save the time of writing individual notes that all bear the same message – I believe the plague of inattentiveness is that great. Not that it's new. Back in the nineteenth century, psychologist and philosopher William James wrote: 'The faculty of bringing back a wandering attention over and over again is the very root of judgment, character, and will.'

It is interesting that a problem of near-epidemic proportions, easily diagnosed in children, is almost never perceived the same once adulthood is reached. You'll find few employee appraisal forms that show 'inability to pay attention' as a common problem with staff. And if you ask marriage counselors to rank 'failure to concentrate' in their list of most-heard spousal complaints, the subject probably won't make their lists either.

Once we leave school, the reason for poor performance is usually attributed to a judgement on the poor performance that rarely considers the actual source. Yet I believe that one source of poor performance – the inability to concentrate – is the reason for a host of failures and, more importantly, failed lives. To apply the One and Only Law, you will have to confront your ability to concentrate as much as any other important character trait you have ever tried to improve, because you cannot 'constantly self-confront responsibility' without the ability to concentrate. You see, responsibility becomes what you must concentrate on. For certain people this is the biggest problem in their lives, yet so few realise that this is the source of what is holding them back in life.

If we haven't cured or at least worked on improving our problems with concentration by the time we leave school, I believe we carry with us into the real world one of two 'concentration dilemmas'. See if either of them fits yourself or anyone you know.

The dreamer

This is the case of individuals who are so caught up with what will be in the future that they do not act in the present to make the future happen. While they are often original thinkers and even lucid expositors of their ideas, these people cannot concentrate on the many steps today that are essential to make tomorrow's great leap possible.

It has been my experience that these are among the most creative people around. It is also my belief that their creativity springs, at least partially, from a certainty of failure, a feeling that they will never completely confront their ideas and make them happen. They do not necessarily fear risk but, rather, details; they fear and walk away from the details, details and more details that are the foundation of any idea's growth to fruition. To study and act on details means more concentration than inspiration but this type of person has too much of the latter and not enough of the former. He or she has never really learned to put his concentration to work.

Overactive participant

This is the case of the person who wants to do everything, try everything, and have everything. This type of person, rather than being an idle dreamer, is an overactive participant. He or she always tries – often many things at the same time – and is surprised when success still doesn't arrive. With the quantity of experience and energy applied to a problem also comes the inevitable dilution of quality due to this person's inadequate foundation. Their concentration is dispersed and eventually this shows up in the results. This type of person is usually slow to learn that nobody can do it all or have it all.

Do not despair if you find yourself – at least a past version of yourself – in one of these two concentration dilemmas. It's similar to what happens to us all when we are very young with the world offering its various stimuli and we as children wanting to have it all, do it all – and of course, at the same time. The difference is that winners, at some point, learn to make hard choices, to discriminate about information received, and to home in on specific objectives – yes, to confront responsibility. And the first step is deciding exactly what they want.

I believe that it is more difficult 'bringing back a wandering attention over and over again' now than it was when James wrote his commentary, simply because of the information explosion that we all live with today. Because of the increasing amounts of information we are all subjected to, it is expected that we can absorb more data and that we can perform more tasks in our work and learning environments. Consider the following:

- How many pupils do their homework in front of the television, radio, etc?

- How many drivers tap a foot to the beat of the music coming from the car's speakers?

- How many people on the phone at work start another conversation if they've been put on hold for more than ten seconds?

There are times when it is difficult and almost impossible to concentrate effectively: when you are feeling tired, bored, anxious or unmotivated. During these times you must overcome what is preventing your mind from concentrating or you will inevitably:

1. Perform in a mediocre manner.
2. Take twice as much time to accomplish your task.
3. Fail at what you are attempting to do.

Concentration is something that every winner, in his or her own way, must learn to do, without exception. For some it can be a learning process that is lifelong, with a constant battle to restrain one's 'wandering attention'. But being able to successfully concentrate reaps four major benefits that cannot be ignored.

1. Concentration allows you to focus on what you want

By giving focus to one item or area in your life and temporarily shutting out other subjects, winners are able to sharpen their minds quickly. This state of high concentration is generally self-induced, but in some cases circumstances can bring the concentration to you.

Novelist Joseph Heller (*Catch-22* and other works) was immobilised for five months and partially paralysed for two years when he was stricken with Guillain-Barre syndrome in 1981. In *No Laughing Matter*, he wrote this of his recuperation:

> I could not remember a time in my life, in childhood, adolescence, or adulthood, when my vision of what I wanted to accomplish was so uncluttered. I knew where I was and I knew why I was there. My conscience was clear. My children were self-supporting. I felt under no obligation to anyone other than the people who were helping me and those I felt friendly toward. Never in my past had my emotions and my moral life seemed so uncomplicated. My problems were few and I knew what they were. I needed to make money, I wanted to finish my novel, I wanted to get better.[1]

This degree of forced concentration goes beyond (let's hope) the limits most of us will ever face. But Heller's message is to all of us: we have to sometimes unclutter our lives, concentrate on only one thing – what we really want – and take the responsibility for going after it.

2. Concentration creates effort

In professional sports, concentration separates the men from the boys and the women from the girls. Pat Bradley earned more money than any woman golfer (in 1986) after she started practising what she called 'the stare, a trance-like state, a zone of concentration extremely intense and consuming,' according to *People* magazine.[2]

In business, concentration rarely receives the same recognition, but is just as important. American businessman John Reed is an example not only of effort in concentration but of super-concentration. He is dyslexic; that is, he sees letters and numbers scrambled and has to hear words before he can say them. Reed's disability wasn't diagnosed until adulthood, but he learned to concentrate and overcome his ailment – and went on to be one of the world's pre-eminent bankers as chairman of Citicorp. He recently said in an interview, 'If I fail it will be from too long a reach.'[3]

Yet you don't have to be a professional in sport or a top banker to benefit from focused concentration and its results. A friend of mine, a writer with a quick, self-confrontational system for dealing with writer's block, explained his successful technique to me. Whenever blocked, he turns away from the screen of his computer and writes these words on a pad of paper: 'What am I trying to say?' He stares hard at that question until he has his answer, and then returns to the keyboard.

It's always easy for the allure of distraction to prevail, and, as we all know, it is difficult for concentration to be enforced. But it is necessary if you are consistently to win at whatever it is you are striving for.

3. Concentration creates organisation

For those who need better organisation, the ability to concentrate translates into the need to prioritise their tasks and confront at the end of the day what they have actually accomplished. This is because with effective concentration, more tasks you are working on tend to get finished and, therefore, log-jams of work begin breaking up and priorities become important because projects are actually getting completed on time. The huge growth in time-management systems is testimony to the need of so many busy people to concentrate on and improve how they spend their time.

4. Concentration relaxes and renews

Sometimes the best concentration is simply found in serenity, or thinking about nothing at all. Yoga, transcendental meditation, relaxation audiotapes, self-hypnosis and other forms of pro-grammed relaxation meet this need for some people. Others can just take a ten-minute rest without any outside assistance and feel relaxed and renewed. Yet there are those who have a self-changing inner mechanism and recharge themselves without any apparent relaxation. We all need, at one time or another in our busy days, to focus on nothing at all, but with the pressures and distractions of modern life, that can be, for some, difficult to achieve.

The message of this chapter is simple: You cannot confront yourself accurately if you cannot concentrate thoroughly.

How do you confront that? Do you need to change your life in order to accomplish the ability effectively to concentrate? Are you willing to pay the price of giving up something you only partially have in order to focus on something you must have? *There is loss with concentration.* There has to be. It involves choices. Are you ready to choose, and at first to lose, in order to win?

To start, are you ready to look for help in better concentrating? The relaxation and renewal programmes noted on the previous page are available to anyone interested in experimenting in this area. If you are not the kind of person who can achieve high levels of concentration by taking short breaks or who can easily recharge yourself, then examine one or more of the popular self-help programmes that appeal to you most.

Don't waste any more time before confronting the subject of the effectiveness of your own concentration skills. That was what Samuel Johnson might have been implying when he wrote, more than 200 years ago, 'When a man knows he is to be hanged in a fortnight, it concentrates his mind wonderfully!'

Notes

1. Joseph Heller and Speed Vogel (1987) *No Laughing Matter*, Corgi.
2. *People*, 25 May 1987.
3. *Fortune*, 4 January 1988.

> *Only constant self-confrontation of*
> *responsibility reaps results*

Attention and You:

Essential Self-Confrontations

- Have you learned to pay attention, to be able to concentrate on what you want?

- Have you learned to relax and renew yourself in spite of the pressures you face?

- Are you ready to take action if you've answered 'no' to either of the above questions?

- What specific action will you now immediately take today?

CHAPTER 12

Change: Real Power is Portable

Of all the quotations I've seen or heard about the changes that will transform our world over the next few decades, I have a special fondness for the following: 'The majority of new jobs created in the next twenty years will come from companies not yet created and for products and services not yet invented.' This is the only quotation in the book whose source I cannot verify. What I like about it is that it doesn't matter whether you or I believe it, because it can't be comprehended. Such a prediction can only be absorbed with a gulp or a smile.

Will change be a benevolent light at the end of our proverbial tunnel of darkness? Or will the light really be the headlights of a train coming the other way to run us down? I don't know. You don't know. No one knows for sure.

The only thing we do know is that significant change is under way, that it has affected and will continue to affect individuals and families, jobs and careers – more profoundly than anything we have seen in the past five decades and maybe, if we believe the extremists, in the past 200 years.

Test yourself about this easily, right now. Are you doing the same job for the same employer with the same responsibilities, and in the same environment, as you were five years ago? Do you have the same goals, personal and career, as you had five years ago? Do you have the same spouse/love interest as five years ago?

Few things are the same as they were five years ago. In this the information age, five years is history.

The information revolution is leading to more change, more often, for more and more people. There are some very tough questions for you to consider. Do you have a habit of sending out radar and sensing change that will affect you? If you can't predict change, can you at least project change that might come your way, to your industry, and be ready to adapt? Although you may already be acting from strength, have you considered the possibility that it might have to be redirected? For example, if you are an engineer and an administrative function arises within your company that allows you to broaden your scope of experience, would you go for it?

Are you not only acting from strength but expanding from it? That is the confrontation of this chapter. Is the power you have in your work – be it experience, credentials, authority, talent, education – portable to another environment, another company, another industry? If change hits you negatively, will you be ready to move?

William Shakespeare wrote in *Julius Caesar*: 'There is a tide in the affairs of men, which, taken at the flood, leads on to fortune.' However, he omitted to write that the same 'flood' can drown you if taken at the wrong time or if not paid attention to at all. Let there be no doubt about it: There is some very high water coming.

Into the fray of the future we will all swim or drown, and I make this observation of the differences from a career/opportunity viewpoint and a personal-relationship viewpoint. Every industry, profession, and trade will probably be affected differently by change, and every personal relationship not necessarily differently but certainly more intensely. You have only to look at the world of business to see that there is no single blanket solution for any industry or business within an industry. Some will prosper only with the highest technological investments, others by innovating in the simplest, most basic areas of customer service or by meeting the latest fashion trend.

When Tandem Computers, after a four-year slump, saw earnings rocket by 80 per cent in 1987, chief executive officer Jimmy Treybig credited that change to his own transformation in management style. He changed from being a 'one of the boys' manager to a tough, bottom-line manager. 'I used to be a cheerleader. Now I'm a manager,' he said.[1]

Robert Greenberg, founder and president of LA Gear, Inc, found that regularly posing as a sales clerk in one of his busy Los Angeles shoe shops on Saturday mornings gave him the information he needed to shape his trendy, athletic footwear company. 'I learn more about my business from those three hours a week than anything else,' he affirmed.[2]

What both these examples demonstrate is that it is better to confront change early than be overwhelmed by it later. In my own small, special-project advertising agency I try, in my own way, to use this radar effect as much as Greenberg or Treybig. Every morning, I study the list of current projects and, after assessing the status of each, consider what the worst possible scenario for each could be and what action I would take if that were to occur. Am I being negative? Not at all. I'm just trying to stay ahead of surprises and be ready to move quickly. By just considering possible bad news it can sometimes be avoided. It's interesting to note that one thing I have never spent time anticipating was what to do with good news.

What are you specifically doing to stay ahead of change in your work?

Personal values, morals, and basic desires for peace, prosperity and security will not change. But – and it's an important 'but' – I believe the stress from change in other areas of life, plus the increasing desire for individual achievement and personal gain, will see personal relationships strained even more in the years ahead.

Anticipating change is not just something to use in your work. The application of this approach to your personal life – anticipating change in those closest to you – can be just as useful in your personal relationships as it can be in your business career. Your wife/husband/lover/child/parent/friend/colleague will be a different person tomorrow than today. Something happens every day to create change in each of us; yet the tendency in all of us to operate out of habit or from preconcieved notions, of positioning a person in our minds to be a certain way, argues against accepting change in others. It is even more difficult to go looking for it. Yet we must or, at least, should, open up our personal radar to hear the beeps of change coming from those closest to us – or else risk growing further and further apart.

For the final quotation on change I defer to the dean of business writers, Peter F Drucker. In the *Harvard Business Review* he recently wrote an article on 'The Coming of the New Organization'. It dealt with change in business and how the successful company of the future may well resemble a hospital or a symphony orchestra rather than the typical organisation we see today, simply because the primary management function will be dealing with information. He wrote:

> Information responsibility to others is increasingly understood, especially in middle-sized companies. But information responsibility to oneself is still largely neglected. That is, everyone in an organization should constantly be thinking through what information he or she needs to do the job and to make a contribution.[3]

I believe the same thought can be applied to not only an organisation, but a career or ambition, a couple or a family. For maximum success, you must have constant, updated information on the forces of change coming into your life. It is a responsibility not to be taken lightly if you want to compete effectively.

Notes

1. *Fortune*, 25 May 1987.
2. *Fortune*, 7 March 1988.
3. *Harvard Business Review*, January/February 1988.

> *Only constant self-confrontation of*
> *responsibility reaps results*

Change and You:

Essential Self-Confrontations

- Do you seek out information that will change your approach to your job or business?

- Are you not just acting from strength but expanding from it by using information to adapt to change by considering another job or organisation, if necessary?

- Do you use your personal radar to discover changes occurring in the people closest to you?

CHAPTER 13

Communication: Perceptions are Perfections . . . and More

Have you ever looked into a mirror unexpectedly and been at least slightly surprised, if not shocked, at the reflection of yourself that stared back?

I have.

Have you ever had your voice recorded without your knowledge, and when played back, said to yourself, 'That can't be me'?

I have.

Have you ever appeared on television or videotape and wondered if that image you saw of yourself was really you?

Again, I have.

Unless you are a pure narcissist, at some point in your life you have seen or heard yourself and felt that something was wanting; you can't believe you really are like that, and if you are, you think you shouldn't be like that. It's because, well, because you're not what you should be . . . because, admit it now, some part of you, at some time, believes that you should be perfect.

Perfect for you is not perfect for me, or for anyone else. It's a personal perfection, a perfection of everything you are when your mind and your body are in complete synchronisation.

Where does it come from?

It has been said that self-image is not what you believe of yourself or what others believe of you. It is what you believe others believe of you. Television has, I believe, very effectively given us the images wherein we are able to define ourselves to others. The dictates of what society wants most are constantly seen there and mixed with what we believe we are, and a self-image is formed. It truly is an image of how others should see us – how we are in our minds when unexpected mirrors, tape recorders and video cameras don't betray that otherwise perfect image.

I do believe we all hold in our minds that hard-to-achieve perfect image of ourselves and that it is our most important fantasy because it defines the very best expectations we have of ourselves. When we face up to what we don't like about ourselves and change, we help ourselves immensely. This could range from a new hair style to capping a tooth to losing weight. Those who ignore this self-image or pay it fleeting attention obscure its potential to help us grow. Those who take perfection to the extreme and overindulge that image in the mirror – to the point of believing that they must always appear perfect to others – do worse. When we end up putting others' opinions above our own beliefs, we rob ourselves of our individuality and identity.

Those who do perfect the image – that total image of how we communicate with looks, words and gestures – and change what they find wanting, have made an important beginning, a first confrontation of their effectiveness in communication. But this is only the beginning. What's just as important is what is usually not confronted: *whether the communication we send is the communication that's received.*

In case you should think that such a confrontation only applies to politicians, salespeople or those who deal frequently with the public, let me assure you it does not. We must all not only be good at what we do but we must be credible. Others must believe that we are that good because of how we communicate who we are and what we do.

We are to others what we appear to be.

Debra Benton is president of the highly successful Benton Management Resources, a training company based in Fort Collins, Colorado. At her seminars, according to recent magazine article, she teaches 'stuffed-shirt executives how to shine'.[1] In her seminar workbook, the article reported, is a funny and profound cartoon. A palm reader is perusing the extended hand of an awesomely uncharismatic executive. 'You are fair, compassionate, and intelligent . . . but you are perceived as biased, callous, and dumb.' The cartoon sums up the problem perfectly: our sterling inner-qualities don't always come across.

What is true about stuffed-shirt executives is just as true about everyone else. Few understand the integrated nature of all our communications and why our sterling qualities just don't always come across.

A few years back, I was very active in speech consulting with business executives and in writing their actual speeches. As I met senior executives for the first time, a familiar scenario repeated itself: they all wanted to know, more than anything, whether I could help them to win a standing ovation with their speech. (This was partly because Standing Ovation was the name of my firm.)

I told the enquiring executive that I would ask him a few questions, and within 15 minutes of listening and probing would have the answer. When asked how I would know within just 15 minutes, I replied that the words I would write for them would be very important but not the largest contribution to the standing-ovation process. The larger parts would be the executive's own interest in the subject, his passion for the opportunity at hand, and the time he was willing to devote to it. These are what would make the words work. In 15 minutes, I said, I would have an assessment of these factors and a forecast that would be highly accurate.

It was extremely interesting to see the reactions of most of the executives. Almost all were caught off-guard at my assessment of their own required contributions. These were seasoned executives with proven leadership skills, winners in the corporate world, yet most of them viewed the opportunity of a speech as a process of having the right words to say. Maybe they were just hoping it was that simple.

In any person-to-person communication, having the right words to say is important, but not more important than saying the right words the right way. And both are not as important as communicating with the right non-verbal communication skills.

It is possible to give a simple breakdown of how we communicate, person to person:

- the actual words you use in communicating with people have a total impact value of 20 per cent;

- how you use words has a value of 25 per cent;

- everything else, 55 per cent: what you wear, how you walk, how you look, your gestures and mannerisms, habits, energy level, and basic social skills.

So, little things do mean a lot. We are all paid on the commission of our credibility.

Only you know when you are close to communicating that perfect image that you carry around in your head and that you see reflected back to you in unexpected situations. No one else knows or cares. Most people only know you for what you present yourself as, not who you really are or hope to be.

Consider, for example, a statistic I've seen that indicates 40 per cent of American adults consider themselves to be shy. American shyness expert and author Jonathan Cheek has said: 'In approaching just about anything, including their careers, shy people don't play to win; they play not to lose. They hesitate to take risks.'[2]

Being shy is not a crime, but if you are shy and yet ambitious in any venture in which other people will judge your performance – and few don't – shyness is not just a trait, it's a message. Writer Pam Withers, in an article about the effect of business people suffering from shyness, told a poignant story of one shy executive. Laid off in a company reorganisation, on the day he was leaving the man casually explained to his supervisor's boss a major breakthrough for the company that he was personally responsible for. This was news to the executive, who had no idea of the man's real value to the company. The general manager of the employment counselling company advising on who to keep and who to 'let go', said that he 'had never taken any onus on himself to let his boss's boss know what he was doing. He felt it wasn't his place to talk to him. He was the easiest person to let go, I think, because . . . they simply figured that he would not put up a fight.'[3]

Shyness is simply one example of a basic communication problem. There are those who are just the opposite: overbearing and boisterous and having this communication problem is just as disastrous to winning as being shy. In all cases, something can be done to improve ourselves, but so many people don't recognise their particular problem. It is difficult, certainly impossible, to see yourself exactly as other people see you, but it is important that you realistically assess the difference, if any, between that image you have of yourself in your mind and what any audience that judges you really sees. The difference will probably be a lot less subtle than the examples stated above, but the likelihood of an inaccurate self-image is quite high.

- Could you believe you are communicating 'friendliness' and an audience is receiving 'scatterbrained'?

- Could you believe you are communicating 'honesty and integrity' and an audience is receiving 'tactless and stupid'?

- Could you believe you are communicating 'creative genius' and an audience is receiving 'strange weirdo'?

- Could you believe you are communicating 'intellectual' and the audience is receiving 'snob'?

Make the following measurements of your own behaviour. First, simply talk to someone who knows you well about how you come across to people. Ask them to choose three or four adjectives to describe you. Select someone whose judgement you trust and ask him or her to be frank. Then, don't just trust his or her answers. Go to a second, a third and a fourth person. Consider the common mosaic they present and you may very well see a picture of yourself that is quite different from what you expected. But don't trust this, either.

If you are really motivated you should buy a copy of an extraordinarily good book on the subject of communication perception and reality: *Molloy's Live for Success*, by John T Molloy.[4] I know it sounds like another of the many inspirational success books out there, but it isn't. It presents a thorough analysis; it's backed up by formidable research about how people communicate, what works and what doesn't. You may be quite surprised at what you find in it. While the book is written for business people, its findings can be used by anyone.

But that isn't enough either – not if you have any serious doubts about yourself. If your company has a personnel department, ask them if they can recommend a psychologist who can provide communication assessment. If this isn't possible, find one yourself.

Not accurately understanding how you are perceived is no indictment of your character, talent or ability. It is simply a misperception. And this misperception can be very costly to your future success in life.

Katharine Hepburn, on looking back on an acting career that can be called nothing less than illustrious, recently said:

'For years and years I thought an audience had come to say, "There she is, the silly thing. She's been so goddam lucky, you know. And she is not much good. She doesn't know what she is doing. We're going to kill her."'[5]

If someone with the talent and stature of Katharine Hepburn could communicate memorable, dramatic performances while living with such a terribly inaccurate misperception, there is room for all of us to consider whether the message we think is being communicated is the message being received.

I know that this is an easier confrontation to read about than to do anything about. It's even easier to dismiss, since you have a pretty good idea of what that image in the mirror says to others. At least you believe you do.

In this area, belief alone is too dependent upon your past and potentially harmful to your future. Consider your entire method of communication a science, not a faith – a science in need of exploration. And consider what the late Richard Feynman, the Nobel Prize-winning physicist, said about his science:

'The first principle is that you must not fool yourself – and you are the easiest person to fool.'[6]

Notes

1. *Chatelaine*, January 1989.
2. *en Route*, Air Canada, May 1988.
3. Ibid.
4. John T Molloy (1984) *Molloy's Live for Success*, Bantam.
5. *Newsweek*, 31 August 1987.
6. *Time*, 26 December 1988.

> *Only constant self-confrontation of*
> *responsibility reaps results*

Communication and You:

Essential Self-Confrontations

- Do you ever confront the image you wish to communicate to people?

- Have you made any necessary changes to make sure that you are pleased with the person you see in the mirror?

- Do you try to perfect this image so that it's everything you want it to be without putting others' opinions ahead of your own?

- Have you tested the message that you believe you are sending? Is it definitely the same message that's being received?

CHAPTER 14

Thinking: The Wisdom of Investigation, Imagination and Ignorance

There is a wonderful irony in the very idea of reading about and thereby thinking about the process of thinking. Thought is the one activity that every human being engages in more than any other, yet we're not taught how to do it.

Not only that. We really don't think about not being taught how to think.

The confrontation I'm asking you to make in this chapter is this: do you think in a manner that is beneficial to enforcing the One and Only Law of Winning?

Before answering, let me suggest that you may be going about answering this the wrong way. It is my observation that winners, regardless of talents or traits, share a specific yet individually twisted process involving three stages in their thinking processes: investigation, imagination, and ignorance. Before I go on to explain these processes, let me first ask you to consider the fundamental and basic process of thought itself.

Except for the rocket scientists among us, who think in the perfect abstraction of numbers, most of us think – and by that I mean consider, plan, evaluate, decide, write, report, speculate and so on – with language. And language is learned after other learning has taken place: the basic motor skills from moving our hands to crawling and walking. Language is learned the same way, by remembering what we've already learned, adding to it, evaluating it, and practising it.

What the preceding and admittedly ultrasimple definition of

the thought process is meant to establish is that most thinking is highly experientially based. We consider what will happen from a base of experience or proof of what has happened in the past. We wouldn't want to touch a hot stove too many times before learning not to repeat the experience. Experiential thinking does pay off.

This type of thinking is encouraged more than any other type. Has there been a more quoted dictum in recent years than poet-philosopher George Santayana's 'Those who cannot remember the past are condemned to repeat it'? There is no better proof of the esteem in which we hold experiential learning than the high regard we have for economists. These forecasters of future economic performance formulate their theories of what will happen from various economic models based upon past experience. We accept their predictions due to their rational, experiential explanations, because they formulate their theories the same way we formulate our own – unlike mystics and other soothsayers, whose predictions are not experientially based.

Yet most governments, corporations or individuals do not expect the predictions of economists to be completely accurate. We accept their forecasts as the best that can be taken from experiential projection. The economists who do their work competently, who accurately predict recessions, expansions or stock-market gyrations, are hailed as gurus. Imagine if the same criteria were applied to other occupations. Would a headline scream, 'Plumber Fixes Six Leaky Taps in a Row' or 'Window Cleaner Actually Completely Cleans Window'? Of course not. We forgive economists for not being accurate with their forecasts because we believe they do the best they can with a very murky and unreliable raw product: past experience.

To enhance and focus the process of thinking, I believe it is both necessary to accept and reject the evaluation of experience as being murky and unreliable. It certainly is both when used alone – and that is how many, many people use it, projecting it before them as a battle tank of truth, rather than what it is: one person's collected best judgements, feelings, and beliefs about the past. But when experience is viewed differently, as an inventory of various performances, not a collective judgement, you can pluck from this inventory true, priceless treasures and apply them, together with the three other stages of the thinking process – investigation, imagination and ignorance – to understand not only the act but the true art of thinking.

Let's look at these three stages of the thinking process and see how they can work together with experience.

Ignorance

You may think that ignorance is not a resource but a state of mind, and you already know too many people with this affliction and would do anything rather than join them. This is understandable. Ignorance has got a bad name from people who are not only ignorant but insensitive and boorish. Any two of the three are a bad combination, but ignorance by itself is really innocence, meaning 'without knowledge'. That's the way most of us frequently find ourselves facing the various predicaments of life. (Not that we often admit it.)

The first human response to any challenge is not to think but to react. Psychologists tell us we all have a 'fight or flight' response built into our genetic structure: a response literally to run like hell or put up a stern verbal, and possibly even physical, fight because once in our evolutionary history this was the only way we solved our problems.

Today, many people still solve their problems this way, by living on the edge of frustration or anger, by using the battle tank of their past experiences to validate each righteous response with anger, accusations and so on. This approach does not use thought. It relies upon reaction.

Ignorance for winners, usually, is the first process in thinking. It stops us from reacting (except in life-threatening or other dangerous situations) and allows us to say to ourselves, 'I don't know the answer to this situation but I'd better think it through.' Using the resource of ignorance sometimes means scratching your head when you first consider complicated options or sometimes saying to a person who brings you unsettling news, 'What you're saying is . . .' And then you play back the news you've just heard in your own words.

Using ignorance to your advantage is admitting that your brain

115

is not a bank of wisdom from which withdrawals can be made instantly, but that it can be a wisdom-producing machine if the process of thinking is given a chance to function at full capacity. This is a challenge for all of us because we want to believe the opposite, that with all we've been through in life, there ought to be a warehouse full of wisdom to be dispensed. Occasionally there is, but this is too infrequent an occurrence to be relied on. It almost never harms you, in any complicated situation, to say, at least to yourself, 'I don't know', and give the full thinking process a chance to function.

There are no better examples of this than doctors and salespeople. Even if a doctor, upon seeing a patient, his tenth patient with flu symptoms that day, believes in the first 30 seconds that this patient also has the flu, he still goes through the procedure, asks the important questions, listens and looks for symptoms that are different, orders tests if necessary. As much as his experience and his intuition all say, 'Flu', he doesn't accept that judgement until it has been validated. Every examination begins with ignorance and ends with knowledge. That's the way it is.

In a way, the thinking function isn't that different with successful salespeople than it is with doctors. Every person who sells successfully knows that you never successfully sell a prospective customer or convince them of anything by disagreeing with them. Customers buy when you provide the right information in the right way and at the right time – information that lets them add on to what they already believe in order to achieve what they want to achieve. And you must do that better than the next person. More than any other tool, the successful salesperson uses ignorance. He asks questions and he listens, listens, listens – and then listens some more. He interjects only for clarity and makes his presentation only when he knows that he is adding to information the customer already believes.

Your life and work and mine are no different from those of doctors or salespeople in the sense that ignorance must play a fundamental constructive role in how we think. Its importance cannot be overstated.

Imagination

One could argue here that imagination is really part of the creative process and exists by itself, quite apart from rational thinking. I don't believe this because I don't accept that thinking should always be rational. To enhance and use imagination means ignoring the information that your past experience and judgement are telling you is certain. You have to ask yourself the creative questions that lead to uncertain answers: 'Are there any other ways of looking at this?' 'What if?' 'What would I do if I had the same problem but had just arrived from another planet and didn't know what I know?' and similar questions.

Scientist Albert Einstein once wrote: 'Imagination is more powerful than knowledge.' I can't help believing he wrote those words with the insight that imagination, when acting in concert with other thinking resources, creates knowledge. The challenge for us is not to abdicate the use of this resource (imagination) to the arts and sciences but to use it whenever we can in daily life, to make it an integrated part of our thinking process. It is certainly at the heart of our planning processes; we all need a vision of what we want before we can achieve it. But it can also be at the heart of the thought process in everyday and basic thinking. You'll soon see examples of how.

Investigation

There is a very simple test you can give yourself to discover whether you are investigative in your thinking. Picture any problem or opportunity you face as a crime that must be solved by a detective. As much as experience gives your detective insight into the motivation of the criminal, the detective must still sort through many disparate pieces of information to solve the crime. He must investigate without judgement.

Investigation means getting meaningful information that lies beyond your own experience and knowledge. There is a significant problem with the integration of investigation in the thinking process: It slows it down. It's so much easier to search for information within our own knowledge and experience, and to trust our own gut instincts, intuition and imagination, than it is to say, 'I need more meaningful information.'

When I see the hard statistics that four out of five new businesses don't survive five years, I see the triumph of imagination over investigation, of hope over reality. The same can be said of many failed marriages, business and professional partnerships, inventions and other inspired ideas. It is certainly easier to envisage success – being at the top of the ladder – than to consider all the slippery steps that can cause you to fall during the climb. It is not always easy and there's not always time to investigate during the creative thought process. But when you do, you usually think better.

As I wrote at the beginning of this chapter, the integration of these resources into the function of thinking is individually determined. There is no formula. Upon examination, however, we can all see the advantage of integrated thinking over the compulsiveness of quick reaction, a thought process that allows the three extra resources to be used. Let's look at some examples.

Example 1

Have you ever thought that clothing wears out too quickly and that with all the technology at our disposal, someone should invent clothes that last longer? Alex Tilley thought that. He actually went further and invented a hat that repels rain and mildew, is unshrinkable, machine-washable and ties on. It even floats, and he gave it a lifetime guarantee. It was a great success and he started his own company, Tilley Endurables, to sell his remarkable hats from a store in Toronto, Canada.

Tilley saw there was demand for other clothing of the same quality, and envisaged a niche market for adventure clothing with remarkable guarantees. Before his unique hat idea, Tilley had never been even remotely connected with the clothing and textile business and he knew he had to learn a lot quickly. He could not spend much time and money researching the numerous material options for the other clothing he was planning to make as he had for his hat, or he would surely go broke. He was spending all his time marketing and promoting his line of hats and extensive research was just out of the question. In a single, brilliant stroke,

Alex Tilley phoned the Pentagon in Washington, DC, and after much transferring from department to department, was directed to the chief clothing consultant to the military. The consultant told him the results of US Army tests on the strength, durability, and comfort of various fabric combinations.

Today Tilley Endurables Inc, is a multimillion-dollar clothing business that is thriving in both Canada and the United States. Adventurecloth is a Tilley-registered name and although Tilley Endurables clothing bears no resemblance to standard army fatigues, he learned enough technical information in that one phone call to move quickly with various new items into the clothing market-place.

Consider the process involved with Tilley's thinking that led to his phone call. He started with ignorance and no experience – he didn't know what combination of clothing fabrics would last longest. He moved on to investigation, to find out. And last, he made the imaginative and bold leap of asking the consultant to the organisation that buys the most similar type clothing – clothes that have some of the toughest specifications in the world – the U.S. Army. Ignorance, imagination, and investigation – they worked well for Alex Tilley.

Example 2

This example comes from my own life. I am going to share the thought processes with you as they occurred, since the details are such that they could easily be obscured if I simply review them later.

In the autumn of 1988, my youngest son started an afternoon nursery class at our neighbourhood nursery school. But my wife and I wanted him in a morning class, just as he had been the year before, because he suffers from a hearing loss ailment that makes learning more difficult, and mornings were his optimal learning time. But a morning class was not available. When we learned that, two weeks into the school year, classes were to be rearranged and a morning class was going to become available, my wife immediately sent a note to the headteacher. It reminded him of our son's special needs and requested that he be placed in the new morning class. My wife then visited the headteacher to make sure he got her note. She explained our son's adverse reactions during the two weeks' afternoon classes. While his behaviour in class had been fine, he fell apart when he came home and he was not a happy child.

A week later, my wife phoned the headteacher and he told her that he had decided to leave our son in the afternoon class because there were already more students in the morning class than in the afternoon and, the less disruption in classes, the better it would be for the students. He added that he had checked with our son's teacher, who reported that he seemed fine there. His decision was final.

My wife's reaction was shock, and so was mine. My instinctive initial reaction was to confront the headteacher directly, as an outraged parent. Didn't he know that my son had special needs?

But it didn't take me long to remember that in applying the principles of the One and Only Law of Winning you should only confront yourself and your problems and opportunities. The principal had solved his problem, that of placing students in classes. He unfortunately did not solve mine. The assessment that my son should be in the morning class was my problem, not his. Therefore, it was my responsibility to find another acceptable solution after the obvious simple solution of requesting a change did not work.

I immediately went into my ignorance mode and said to myself that I don't know how to solve this – yet. Then I called on my past experience. My shock, I realised, was the result of the high expectations I had of the headteacher. I had known him for five years and believed him to be an excellent educator. Then I found a degree of empathy with him. He had 500 students and was expected to always make the right decision about each one of them. No one was perfect. Couldn't he be excused a mistake? Yes, I reasoned, as long as it was corrected.

So my problem was simplified. I simply had to point out an obvious mistake and have it corrected. But how?

Next came the investigative mode. What meaningful information was out there that I could use? My wife phoned our son's doctor who was in complete agreement that any child with my son's hearing impairment should learn at an optimal learning time and this was obviously important to his proper development. He also provided a letter to that effect. Next, we did a little research and looked into the school's board of governors list of educational priorities. We found that 'meeting the developmental needs of children' was a priority of the board. Further investigation showed that one of the board members in our area had been very involved with research in the area of developmental needs, and we also discovered that another local board member was the current chairman. It also happened to be an election year. This was all good, basic investigation.

Next, I moved into my imagination mode. I imagined that if I sent a letter to the local education authority that calmly and clearly documented the facts, and included our doctor's letter, the error would probably be corrected. I further imagined that if, in the letter, I challenged the authority members to make a public explanation of what priorities superseded the 'developmental needs of children', then, should the error still not be corrected, I would almost surely then have the error corrected. Well, that is exactly what I did, and four days later my son was in the morning class, the error corrected.

If this chapter offers you a single insight, it is this: *how you think – your attitude – is not nearly as important as the resources you think with*. Integrated thinking that harnesses the personal resources of ignorance, investigation, and imagination will almost always lead to a better conclusion than the alternative. This is because it forces you to confront your own responsibilities to the challenge or problem at hand. In every way, every time.

But I caution you that time does not allow us the luxury of applying all three processes all the time. Sometimes you'll go with a hunch, with no investigation. Other times, experience will overwhelm ignorance. Integrated thinking does require time, and when something is important to you, I urge you to practise the law with the three extra resources of ignorance, investigation, and imagination.

> *Only constant self-confrontation of*
> *responsibility reaps results*

Thinking and You:

The Essential Self-Confrontation

- Do you employ integrated thinking that allows you to add ignorance, investigation and imagination to experience in your thinking process?

CHAPTER 15

Conflict: Decongest it before it Consumes You

What is the one thing even a winner can't win? It is simply this: an argument. The reason is equally simple: the one thing that everyone hates to lose is 'face'.

The above paragraph is what I call a self-evident and rational truth. Who can argue with it? And if this were a rational world, I would add that winners never rant and rave, never despair or scream invectives. In a rational world, winners would present themselves passionately but politely, quietly observe the chaos around them, and comment with only the driest wit at the folly of others. And no, they wouldn't argue.

But this isn't a rational world and some winners do vent their anger emotionally – sometimes loudly, and even with little regard for the feelings of others. The reason is not to win an argument – winners know that is not possible. Winners occasionally unleash whatever steam that is necessary for one simple reason: they know it is necessary to resolve and control conflict rather than let conflict become a fire of rage that controls them.

This is seldom easy, but always necessary. Conflict breeds resentment and, as German philosopher Friedrich Nietzsche observed some hundred years ago, 'Nothing on earth consumes a man more quickly than the passion of resentment.'

This chapter asks you to confront, in a tough and tactical way, what you read in Chapters 3 and 4 about your beliefs on the subjects of blame and failure.

Conflicts have two basic sources: (a) the natural competition of people, products, services, and ideas; and (b) the clashes of people through power, politics, personalities and priorities. While

I realise there is some overlap, I believe it is important to examine and understand these sources separately.

Competition and conflict

Yes, competition spurs innovation, and reduces costs of products and services through greater efficiencies. Competition is the heart of enterprise, the very soul of much that is defined as winning. There are, however, two down-sides that relate to competition. The first is the expected: obviously not all competitors win and, when there's loss, there can be recriminations. No one wins all the time. As long as conflict exists within the struggle to win, it is a positive force that brings out the best in people and companies. When it's a judgement, or rather a condemnation of what has happened, watch out for bitterness. You have to learn and move on.

The second down-side is less obvious but just as important to watch out for: Some people confuse 'winning' with 'defeating'. When your focus is on the other person losing instead of on yourself winning, the results can be disastrous and lead to wasting energy on more conflict than can be resolved. Some years ago I had a client in a business which was being outdated by changing technology. He ignored the change all around him and instead of revamping his outdated technology and business practices, he concentrated his energies on putting his main competitor out of business. He accomplished that, and promptly followed his competitor into bankruptcy two years later. This man never really understood how he could lose with his competitor vanquished. He then faced the greatest conflict of all: unresolved conflict of the reasons for failure within himself over the years.

Winners respect competitors. They work against them, yes, but they don't hate them. They use them to keep themselves on their toes and at the cutting edge.

Personal conflicts

People are different. That three-word truth sums up why there is so much conflict around us. In truth, the world and all of us in it probably know more about the people conflict than we do about human cooperation. These conflicts among ourselves must be confronted and dealt with in order to clear the path to winning.

As a trainee in one of my early jobs I had a colleague who was supposed to supervise my training. She did this by belittling me personally over every mistake I made. After a few weeks, I confronted myself on the need for a change. In a private conversation with this colleague I pointed out that her manner was unacceptable. I suggested that if she could not point out my mistakes objectively and not personally, she should tell the manager that she could not do the job. She was taken aback, said very little, but her attitude changed from that day and we worked together well until I was promoted into a different department.

In *Swim With the Sharks Without Being Eaten Alive*, Harvey MacKay tells the story of a conflict with a former business associate that went on for half a decade. 'The psychic energy and accumulated bitterness that went into my thoughts of revenge consumed me for the better part of five years.'[1] He goes on: 'It was more than a waste of time, because whenever I thought about it, I grew vindictive and sour, and those attitudes spilled over into everything I touched. As a result, I lost more than did the object of my revenge.'

Once you confront yourself on the fact that there is a negative conflict in your life, you must face up to it, deal with it, and move on. Winners learn, more than anything else, that life is a process, a moving process, and not a singular event or judgement to focus their days and nights on. But even those who live a fault-free life face the inevitable disappointments caused by some conflicts, and the feelings they arouse must be confronted as real, and dealt with. Whether this means yelling, a long, brisk walk, a quiet talk with a friend; whatever can be done by you that does not harm others (or more importantly yourself) must be done.

There is an old saying, 'Revenge is a dish best eaten cold'. Winners go one better. Revenge is a dish best frozen and forgotten. There are not enough tomorrows for us to squander any on the squalor of our yesterdays.

Note

1. Harvey MacKay (1988) *Swim With the Sharks Without Being Eaten Alive*, William Morrow.

> *Only constant self-confrontation of responsibility reaps results*

Conflict and You:

Essential Self-Confrontations

- Is the focus of your life on the present, what you can do now, or is it on a conflict of the past?

- Have you found your own way of dealing with disappointments caused by conflicts, one that helps you let go and move on?

CHAPTER 16

Authority: It Comes with the Territory

A teenage boy, about to leave an amusement park, remembered a promise to bring a souvenir back for his young sister. He saw a man selling balloons for 50 pence. The boy dug deep into his pockets but only came up with 30 pence, the last of his money. The boy was about to forget the idea when he saw something that changed his mind.

When the man selling balloons had no other customers, the boy approached him. 'Excuse me, sir,' he said, 'I notice you have one balloon that's smaller than the rest – the green one. It's probably losing air. I promised my sister a balloon and I only have 30p – can I buy it?'

The man was not moved. 'Sorry, son. They're all 50 pence. Can't help you.'

'But I promise I won't complain, sir, even if it loses the rest of its air as I walk away.'

'Look son, if these were mine, I'd give you the balloon. But they're not. I'm not authorised to sell any balloon for less than 50 pence.'

The boy did not want to offend the man, but he saw his opening and slyly went for it. 'Yes, sir, but I know you must also be authorised by the park management to give people full value for their money. If you sell that one balloon for 50 pence and it's no good, you won't be providing value. If you take my 30p for it, you will. I promise I won't complain, no matter what happens to the balloon.'

The man looked at the smaller balloon, then smiled at the boy and replied, 'OK, so where's your money?'

The moral of this story is not that persistence overcomes resistance. Nor is it that creative negotiation is usually possible. No, the moral of the story is this: few people realise the full authority they already have.

'How can I take responsibility when I don't have the authority to do so?' you may also ask. This is not so much a question as it is a complaint about organisational structure. The answer to the question and the complaint is the same: be sure of all the authority you do have. You probably have more than you think. And press for any that you need.

You cannot 'constantly self-confront responsibility' unless you believe you have the authority to do so. Authority comes within the territory of responsibility. There are two principal obstacles to authority; one is personal, the other structural.

1. The personal obstacle

This has nothing to do with other people; it only concerns yourself and the authority you believe you have to do what you want.

For many, there is a fixed picture in their minds of who they are that is in conflict with what they want to do. This could be because of an overwhelming influence of a parent early in life – or any number of other reasons. It is similar to, and for some the same scenario as, the person who lacks confidence (see Chapter 6), and the same solution is required. You need information and education to change this perception of yourself. This could be simple or complex, depending on the ambitions you have and the image (or personal obstacle) that prevents them from happening. It could very well involve therapy. My advice for overcoming your personal obstacles is: do what you have to do to give yourself the authority that matches your ambitions.

2. The structural obstacle

This obstacle is different. This is the conundrum of feeling the responsibility to act but being held back by lack of defined authority: by a boss, a committee, even a corporate policy that keeps authority away from your responsibility. This is a common frustration of middle-level managers. The ironic twist to it is that it's the exact opposite of the frustration that senior management feels. When the Atlanta Consulting Group conducted a survey on what makes big-company presidents anxious, the top three items were:

(a) Subordinates' failure to accept or carry out responsibility.
(b) Failure to get critical information.
(c) Firing someone.[1]

While all organisations are different, I believe it can be assumed that responsibility and authority are never precisely aligned. No job description can allow for all the variables, all the problems and opportunities that will arise. Remember: management expects more responsibility, so it is your first responsibility to make sure that you have the authority to do what you have to do. I suggest the following steps:

1. Examine the authority that you now have

Have you overlooked an area? (Remember, the balloon salesman in the earlier example, until it was pointed out to him, didn't realise he had the authority to give people full value for their money.)

2. Ask for clarification from your boss about how your responsibilities are matched by your authority

Don't worry, he or she will know what you really want.

3. Press gently for change

Present a change not in the light of how you'll have more authority, but by emphasising how much more efficiently the department or company will be able to operate. Present yourself as a team player who just wants to make a better play.

The bottom line is that if you don't ask, you won't receive.

If you ask and you don't receive the authority to match your responsibility, you'll have to consider moving to another position or another organisation. In one of my jobs, I remember being astounded by the time the senior management committee of the company spent making the trivial decision about what ranks of manager received the various kinds of company stationery (eg, embossed, personalised, coloured, etc). When I asked my boss how the committee had time for this, he said, 'Bern, they don't know how to solve the big problems of the company. This keeps them busy.' He was right. This was also an indication of the entire power structure and top heavy authority of the company. Over the years it lost many eager managers who were hungry for the authority to match their ambitions.

You need the authority for what you must do. If you don't have it, get it.

Note

1   *Wall Street Journal*, 3 June 1980.

> *Only constant self-confrontation of responsibility reaps results*

Authority and You:

Essential Self-Confrontations

- Do you have the authority to match your responsibilities?

- If the answer is no, is the source of the problem personal or structural?

- Are you prepared to take the necessary action to overcome the problem?

Part 4

Living the Law

This is the hard part. As much as the One and Only Law provides for common areas of faith and practice, the specific details of living the law must be applied individually.

For some this is easier than for others. However, it is necessary for all. I have some final chapters of advice before you take the law into your own hands.

CHAPTER 17

The Difference: Really Deciphering the Law

How many kinds of winner can there be? Potentially there can be as many kinds as there are people; everyone has to win in his or her own personal way. The very definition of the One and Only Law – *only constant self-confrontation of responsibility reaps results* – includes the responsibility of deciding what you will win at. But my examination of the law, how it's obeyed and disobeyed, has led me to my own special confrontation, which I will now share with you: Although there certainly must be individual ways of living the law, winners can be found within the framework of three categories.

How you decipher and apply the law to your own life will be determined in part by the category you find yourself in. Here are the possibilities:

1. The unceasing winner

I know that some winners, like champions, are 'made, not born', but I also confess, after much study of the subject, that some winners are on the fast-track to winning at such an early age that the source of their pursuit cannot easily be defined. These unceasing winners appear before us and amaze us with their appetite for life and their uncompromising style of self-confronting their own responsibilities. Even more, they never doubt, or seem to doubt, what their responsibilities are or that they will be met.

The late Jim Shore was a man I had only heard about, but I had heard about him from the man who gave him his first and only job in advertising. John Burke-Gaffney was general manager of the Cockfield Brown advertising agency in Winnipeg during the 1950s. A very young Jim Shore came and asked him for a job. Shore said that he did not care what he was paid, since he would only be there six months and would then consider assigning Cockfield Brown the advertising account of a new company he and an associate were forming. It would be a brand-new service company, something totally new. Would Mr Burke-Gaffney hire him?

John told me that the young man's enthusiasm and potential offer were irresistible. 'I don't remember what we were paying young account men then, but he didn't care', John recounted. 'He had this idea that his new company would only be successful if he won the most prestigious direct-mail award of the day in its first year of operation, and to do that he would have to know the advertising business inside out. To accomplish that, Jim would have probably worked for nothing if he had to.'

Shore was true to his word. He left the advertising agency after six months and promptly assigned it the advertising account of his new concept in business: a company that would offer other companies temporary office employees. Shore's business, Office Overload, did win the major direct-mail award of its day and went on to be extremely successful.

Think about having an idea for a new company and seeing the need to work, without caring about salary, for six months in order to gain insight into how you will make the new idea work.

The essential aspect of unceasing winners such as Jim Shore is not merely that they are visionaries. Yes, they have dreams, but a lot of people have dreams who are not like them. And it's not just determination or willpower. It's an uncanny combination of talents, ambitions, dreams, a capacity for engaging the details of what has to be done, and certainly the constant self-confrontation of responsibility that this book is all about.

This type of winner is rare, and the essential quality of winning, if not innate at birth, is learned early and applied often.

2. The 'click!' winner

These are people who are far, very far from considering themselves winners until, almost literally, something goes 'click!' in their heads: A psychological metamorphosis is evolved and an entirely new perspective on life and priorities is attained. The 'click!' winner is an instant winner who receives far more in benefits than any instant lottery winner. He or she receives an immediate perspective on what is wrong in his or her life and sets out to correct it with near-missionary zeal. These winners' sense of understanding the law is incredible, as if it had been slowly absorbed but never acknowledged as such until – 'click!' – their lives are set in new motion.

Tony McGilvary was a con man in the US, a career criminal who spent almost 22 years in prison. One of his wardens commented that he didn't think Tony could 'make it on the street himself, let alone help anyone else.'[1] And by all rightful odds, he shouldn't have. But McGilvary not only 'made it on the street' as a responsible citizen, but formed an extremely effective programme for keeping ex-cons out of prison, getting them jobs, and allowing them the chance to become winners themselves. The programme he founded is called HELP, and with extraordinary success it has now aided many thousands of other ex-convicts. McGilvary has been honoured by both government and private industry for his incredible programme.

What changed Tony McGilvary? In the book *Square John* he writes about his prison conversations with a nun, Sister Marguerite, and about one special meeting.

That's when she hit me with the line that made me turn myself around. 'Aren't you tired of hurting yourself, Tony?' . . . Yeah, I was tired, real tired.[2]

Sister Marguerite then commented,

For him, that was the moment he turned it around. For me, that was the day we talked, and that's what enabled him to turn it around. I'll never forget the expression on his face. It reminded me of the quote from Isaiah, 'He was a man

139

acquainted with sorrow.' I'll never forget Tony's sorrowfulness that day.[3]

Yet sometimes the 'click!' – the change, the turnaround – isn't that dramatic. The *New York Times* told the story of two foster parents, Buddy and Emily Kauffman, who exemplify the best of their kind. One of their wards, Kim Thornton, was taken from alcoholic parents, returned to the parents, came back to the Kauffmans – all with typically traumatic results for a girl who from age eight had lived in an alcoholic chaos. The *Times* report about this special child related that in the eighth grade, something clicked in her head that changed her life dramatically. Kim explained:

> 'It's like they say, a child realizes he controls his life. I got the attitude that my parents had their shot, they couldn't handle it, now it's my life, my turn. I started to study really, really hard. I took all that anger and I tried out for basketball.'[4]

The *Times* article follows Kim up to her second year of university, with this quote on her ambition.

> 'I'm going to get an education; I'm going to get a good job. President of the United States, that's my goal. A lot of people say, "Kim, I've never seen a woman President." I may even be a single woman President; I don't know if I'll even be married by then. It's unrealistic, President, but I want goals. I want to change something. I want to put a law through, I want to be a mayor or lobbyist, not just an ordinary person.'[5]

The essential perspective that all 'click!' winners receive is an unerring vision of what they can do, coupled with a firm focus on their own responsibility for attainment. The 'click!' itself is the resolution of a critical, internal conflict. With that resolution come results, because there are then no excuses, only responsibility for results. That is all that they can see.

3. Slouching winners

These don't have the uncontained enthusiasm, the vision, or the persistence of unceasing winners, and they also lack the unerring and focused vision of converted 'click!' winners. These are winners who constantly intellectualise and rationalise life and its meaning. They look for meaning first and winning second, and maybe for them the pursuit of meaning becomes winning.

These are winners who acknowledge the essence of the law, and when push comes to shove, they seize responsibility promptly and reap the results. They then often slouch back to older, easier ways with concepts less challenging than constant self-confrontation of responsibility in front of them. They often leave the word 'constant' out of their own definition of winning.

I know this category of winner well, since it is the category in which I find myself. (You will remember that my discovery of the law was more of a slow crawl than an instant 'click!') You will also find many, if not most, of the people profiled in this book in this category. These are winners who confront their beliefs casually, who challenge practising the law vaguely, until prepared or pressed to do otherwise. Then they do obey the law with a passion for winning. And they do win.

So what kind of winner are you or will you become?

If you are an unceasing winner you know it. You've really known it for a good part of your life. This book will provide you, at best, with a few titbits, a few ideas or considerations to tinker with, to add to your repertoir of life management techniques, to use as you wish. You have long been on your way. I believe few people old enough to read and understand this book can become unceasing winners. The mind-set comes early, very early.

If you are already a 'click!' winner, you've known it since the first chapter – maybe when you first picked up the book. And you haven't just read this book, you've devoured it. You're in a hurry and you devour everything you read. If you are going to become a 'click' winner, it may be that the book will help this happen sooner. It can't create the click. That will come only when you make that big internal confrontation and the reality of what you must do, and why you must do it, appears before you. And it will change your life when it happens.

If you are or will become a slouching winner, you will find this book most appropriate in many ways. It will help you to slouch a little less and stand a little taller, and there's a very specific way to make that happen sooner – as I will explain.

Notes

1. Marlene Webber and Tony McGilvary (1988) *Square John*, University of Toronto Press.
2. Ibid.
3. Ibid.
4. The *New York Times*, 3 January 1989.
5. Ibid.

CHAPTER 18

A Perspective: Where You are Going

Life is only difficult. It is not complicated. Many people lead plagued lives because they cannot make the distinction between those two words. The winds of chance buffet them. Other people's priorities control them. They make no decisions with consistency. They are searching without direction.

Those who live the law do know the difference between 'difficult' and 'complicated'. They understand the motion of life and set a direction. Life, for winners, can be difficult indeed, but it is not complicated. Living the One and Only Law of Winning uncomplicates life. Self-confrontation of responsibility rolls right over complications.

To set a direction, you need a perspective on where you've been and where you're going. If you mentally draw a time line of your life's achievements, with a firm picture of your past accomplishments on the left and your future to your right, you have a perspective on where you are going. Anyone can see where he or she is headed by looking at where they've been. If nothing in your life changes, you can be pretty sure that what will happen on the right side of that picture will not be much different from the left.

A review of the sort of problems you might have will fall into three different categories of problem:

- those that are with you now and will be with you tomorrow because in all likelihood nothing can be done about them – ever;

- those that will go away all by themselves because you unknowingly misperceived their importance;

- those that you should confront and change.

I believe that even comprehensive and enthusiastic plans for change often fail because this simple distinction of problems or opportunities is not made. To concentrate on the first type is to ensure failure (those that nothing can be done about). To care exclusively about the second creates confusion (those that will go away by themselves). The only things you and I can change are the third type (those that you should confront).

The real secrets to setting a new direction for your future effectively are as follows:

1. Observe yourself wanting things. (You'll soon read why and how).
2. Recognise that you must define and differentiate *both* problems to be solved and opportunities to be seized.
3. Be aware of how wrong you often can be.

How to change where you are going

1. The importance of observing yourself wanting things cannot be overstated. It relates to consciousness, our very awareness of life. In today's fast-paced world, often there is too much clutter for all of us; too much happening.

It is frequently difficult to separate a want from a whim, an attainable dream from a lamentable desire, a problem that is real from a problem that is smoke. It is important that you discover this for yourself – so you can better differentiate the things you want that are important, from those that are not.

2. To observe yourself wanting things and recognise the difference between problems and opportunities, I advise you to make a list of your problems, opportunities and desires every month.

Force yourself to include some opportunities, even if they are far-fetched to start with. Otherwise read your list a month later and see how many problems and opportunities are still with you. Then make a new list – and keep doing this each month. In your lists write all the detail you can. Save these lists and study them for a true evaluation of what your problems and opportunities really are. Don't hurry the process. Look for consistency, repetition, a pattern of what must be done, a focus. It will inevitably appear as the whims of your life will disappear.

3. Consider this evaluation and apply it to the time line of your life's achievements that was mentioned at the beginning of this chapter.

Look closely at where you've been, where you're going, what you want, and where you should be going.

Where you should be going may be difficult, but it won't be complicated. You will know – without any doubt – for you will have methodically confronted yourself on your own future. And you will reap the results of confronting that responsibility and redirecting your energies where they are most needed to achieve your own realistic goals.

4. To be aware of how wrong you often can be you need only review the frank information gleaned from parts 1 and 2 above.

Learn from past mistakes or, as the saying goes, you will be doomed to repeat them. Better still, learn of future possible mistakes before you have a chance to make them.

CHAPTER 19

Only You: What You Really Need

I did not invent the One and Only Law of Winning. I just realised that it existed and wrote it down – for myself, for you, and for anyone else who reads this book. In this, the last chapter, I make my final observations on the law and ask you to consider four essential self-confrontations:

1. The law is not fair, never has been and never will be

That's why it's a law of life and not a law of man. It does not concern itself with justice, with what should happen; it concerns itself only with the process of life, what does happen. That's where the law exists, awaiting your active intervention in what is going on around you, your own confrontation of your responsibility. But the law does not wait for long. It lives in time and leaves its judgements after events and non-events alike, on both the responsibilities you do and do not confront. Yet only winners recognise the judgements. Others see only the injustices.

2. The law is not easy

At least not for slouching winners, such as myself. And perhaps you share that category.

If you do, you will find the law something you may frequently avoid but always return to, with luck in the nick of time to confront your next responsibility. It may always be difficult and will never be easy to obey the law. But you will if you believe it, because you will also know that there is no appeal, no higher court.

3. The law is unique

It is the *only* law of winning. While I spent Chapter 2 detailing this, I believe that you may be better prepared to believe me now – after reading the intervening chapters.

The law's pervasive presence in everything we believe and do is truly incredible. The law directs no way out of any situation or problem but forces you to find your way, your best way. You don't have to become anything new that isn't 'you', but the law pushes you to free yourself to find the best you there can be. It is the very heart of every prescription for success because of this. It works for everyone all the time, or against everyone all the time, according to how it is believed and practised.

I am reminded of a television show I saw on which business guru Tom Peters was explaining his frustration at convincing a group of business people that companies like Disney and McDonald's found success in providing consistency of their products and cleanliness in their environments. Peters' frustration grew from the disbelief of the business people. They believed there were other secrets, because 'anyone can do those things'. The fact that anyone can do those things – but few companies do them – was lost on this group. They were looking for secrets that didn't exist.

So it is with the One and Only Law of Winning. Anyone can live it, but, from my experience, few do. Possibly because of its toughness, maybe because of its utter simplicity, probably for a combination of reasons, the law is more often ignored and many people continue to look in other places for secrets of success that do not exist. It's easier than looking inside, at themselves, I suppose.

And now, the last self-confrontation I'll ask you to make . . . and you've seen it before.

4. The law has a heart

Not only is the law, in its entirety, the heart of every system for success, but it has a heart, a core of its own. It is found in Chapter 3, and concerns blame.

You probably understand this by now. If you don't, I ask you to read that chapter again. The degree to which you accept a fault-free life will determine how you will make the law work for you. If you only accept this idea initially, you will be able to win, because you will in time make the other confrontations the law asks of you. 'Fault-free' and 'constant self-confrontation of responsibility' are synonymous. They are the very same thing. This is what you really need.

I did not highlight Chapter 3 with flashing lights, other than to say on its first page that it was the 'essence' of the law, because I wanted you to see this in the context of all the areas of belief and practice that winners share. But I believe I would be remiss in my responsibility to you if I did not confront you on the importance of accepting this idea. And I amplify this critical point with a final thought. It comes from the last sentence in the inaugural address that President John F Kennedy delivered in Washington, DC, on 20 January 1961. Other passages from this speech have been more often quoted, but no quotation from any other source is more appropriate here.

With a good conscience our only sure reward, with history the final judge of our deeds, let us go forth to lead the land we love, asking His blessing and His help, but knowing that here on earth God's work must truly be our own.

This is not just a sentence in a speech. And it's not just about a president leading a nation. It is also about you leading the life you live.

It is also *The One and Only Law of Winning*.

Further Reading from Kogan Page

How to Change Your Life: From Thought to Action, Antony Kidman, 1989

Positive Stress Management: A Practical Guide for Those Who Work Under Pressure, Peter E Makin and Patricia A Lindley, 1991

Successful Self-Management: A Sound Approach to Personal Effectiveness, Paul R Timm, 1988

Tactics for Changing Your Life, Antony Kidman, 1989